Plea...

Emil M

FIKA THAT!
The Swedish Secret
To Coffee, Caring and Connection

Émile Odbäck & Åsa Odbäck

Peaceful Viking
Santa Barbara
Stockholm

PeacefulViking.com

Art by Åsa Odbäck. For more beautiful pieces, or to place an inquiry, visit *AsaKatarina.com*

Cover design by Kris Stuurop
Book Design by Émile Odbäck

To make this book as welcoming and easy-to-digest as possible, we have omitted the citations in text. Please contact us at Info@PeacefulViking.com with any questions, concerns or comments.

ISBN: 978-0-9984459-4-6

For people everywhere who are thirsty for connection & caring!

Special thanks to everyone who helped and supported us along the way. Without your input, research and feedback, this book would never have been possible.

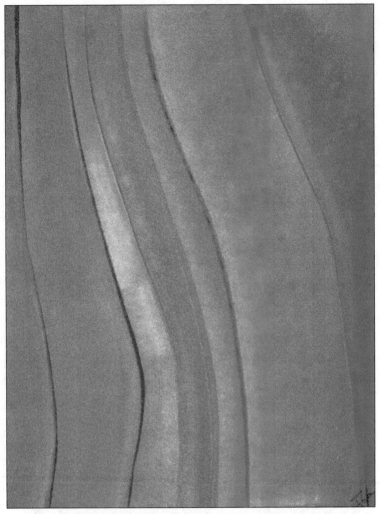

"Too often we underestimate the power of a touch, a smile, a kind word, a listening ear, an honest compliment, or the smallest act of caring, all of which have the potential to turn a life around." *Leo Buscaglia*

Table of Contents

Fika-Foreword

About This (Unique) Book

This book is designed to be an uplifting, inspiring experience, full of energizing stories, engaging quotes, tasty recipes, one-of-a-kind works of art and a whole lot of our own ideas. We've broken the book up into six sections, each designed to motivate you in a unique way — from the History of Coffee all the way to the ABCs of Connection, this book will give you all the tools you need to create your best life, the Swedish way.

The main idea we use to bring all of this to life is Fika — the Coffee break with a Swedish twist that will change your life and the lives of the people around you. One of the most magical things about Fika is that it's not just about improving your own life, but the lives of your family, friends, coworkers, community and, potentially, entire world.

Applying the tips from this book might not cure all the problems in your life, but it most definitely can give you the opportunities and tools to reconnect with yourself and people all over the world. After all, what is more important than that?

Each aspect of this book is designed to give you the tools, understanding and process for incorporating Fika and all of its magic into your life. We want to give you the chance to create your best life starting right here, right now...

It's Not Just Self-Help
It's World Help

These days, it seems like we are all so disconnected from each other. We've moved our focus toward our screens and we've forgotten about the people all around us. Although sometimes it feels natural, this new lifestyle we're collectively creating is incredibly dangerous.

Loneliness, illness, fear, sadness, separation, lack of empathy and even the loss of communication skills are just some of the very real, visible effects of our new, screen-based system of (dis)connection. Even though many of us can see things changing for the worse in our own lives, we don't break out of these patterns because we don't know how, don't have time, are too stressed out, or are just scared to try.

Well, we're here to share the Swedish Secret that just might be the solution...

FIKA THAT!

This book is about having the courage to say "Fika That!" to all the sadness, loneliness, fear and separation that seems to be all around us. This book is about finding solutions to the problems of today together, in a loving, fun, and effective way. But most of all, this book is about the importance of connecting with one-other to recreate a sense of community and oneness in the world.

"Everybody gets so much information all day long that they lose their common sense." *Gertrude Stein*

When we say *Fika That!* we mean, *We're not going to let this stop us or settle for something that doesn't work for us — we're going to overcome, keep going and find the best way.* We hope you will join us in our pursuit of a happier, more connected world and we look forward to sharing a Fika with you soon!

With Love and Coffee,
Émile and Åsa

Section 1:

The Fundamentals of Fika

"A dream you dream alone is only a dream. A dream you dream together is reality."
John Lennon

Small Investment — Big Reward

One day, a young couple finds themselves in great financial trouble. Their business is sinking like the Titanic and their relationship is on its last leg. At last, they decide to ask God for help.

"Please God, help us!" We've lost everything. Please let us win the lottery this week!"

That week's lottery night rolls around... but they do not win.

Again they pray, "Please, oh please God, let us win the lottery this time! Otherwise we are going to lose our house!"

Once again, lottery night comes, yet someone else wins.

For a third time, the couple gets down on their knees and begs, "Please, God, if you can hear us up there in heaven, just let us win the lottery this one time and we will be faithful eternally. We need your help. Please!"

Suddenly, they are overwhelmed by a blinding flash of light, and a deep voice booms out, "Please, you down there on earth, work with me on this! *Buy a lottery ticket!*"

"I would visualize things coming to me. It would just make me feel better. Visualization works if you work hard. That's the thing. You can't just visualize and go eat a sandwich."

Jim Carrey

Take the First Sip

Many of us can relate to the praying couple — we dream of brighter days and better fortune, but we hesitate to take action to actually make our dreams come true. Sometimes, though, our good fortune is just waiting for us to come and get it. One leap of faith, or one moment's worth of focused action, might be just what you need to start living your best life.

Fika is not only cheaper than a lottery ticket, but it also pays out much more often! Each time you choose to connect with somebody, you win. That's the beautiful thing about this practice — there really is no losing, so long as you try.

So, What is Fika?...

"More than a coffee break, Fika is a time to share, connect and relax with colleagues. Some of the best ideas and decisions happen at Fika."

Ikea.com

Fika

Pronounced: Fee-kah

Hard to say... Easy to do!

To Fika means to take a break, connect with people and share some coffee and delicious baked goods. It's a deep-rooted phenomenon — the "Soul of Sweden," as some call it. And, it's a daily fixture in many of the biggest Swedish companies, like Ikea.

Simple • Fun • Effective

Fika is the Swedish phenomenon of taking time to have a good time together — taking breaks to get a breakthrough. Several times each day, coworkers, friends, and families sit down together for 15 minutes to share coffee, treats and conversation. Fika is such an integral part of Swedish society that, like love, it's both a noun and a verb, and also much better when you share it with another person.

"For Swedes, the art of the Swedish 'Fika' in no way compares to a few minutes at the office watercooler, or meeting up with a friend for an espresso in a French cafe. In Sweden, people stop what they're doing to have a 'Fika' at least once a day, sometimes twice."
Thelocal.se

"Swedes prefer not to translate the word Fika. They don't want it to lose significance and become a mere coffee break... Fika is much more than having a coffee. It is a social phenomenon, a legitimate reason to set aside a moment for quality time." *Sweden.se*

It's difficult to say exactly what Fika is because it is so many things!

- It's a time to chat, connect and laugh with old friends, new friends and family.

- It's a moment of relaxation, bliss and comfort in the middle of a hectic day.

- It's a chance to build bridges with all sorts of people, maybe even some you thought were nothing like you.

- It's an opportunity to enjoy some delicious coffee, cookies and conversation.

- It's a friendly, casual, welcoming context for building your circle of friends effortlessly.

- It's revolutionary. It's familiar. It's... Fika.

"Fika is considered a social institution in Sweden; it means having a break, most often a coffee break, with one's colleagues, friends, date or family.... This practice of taking a break, often with a cinnamon roll or some biscuits, cookies, or a fruit on the side, is central to Swedish life." *Wikipedia.com*

MAGNIFIKA!

Far Beyond Coffee

Coffee

Caring

Connection

Community

"Every now and then a man's mind is stretched
by a new idea or sensation, and never shrinks
back to its former dimensions."
Oliver Wendell Holmes Sr.

The Art of Fika: Sit, Sip, Smile!

Fika, at its core is about making people a priority in your life, and making them feel how important they are to you. Although the subtleties and benefits of Fika are extremely complex and far-reaching, the actual process is quite natural.

The ritual of Fika is really as simple as taking a break for 15 minutes and connecting with somebody over a cup of coffee and some snacks. To create a Fika, make some nice coffee (other beverages are okay, but not preferred) and a snack, sit down and turn off all cellphones and computers and connect. The point is to be present and connect with your Fika partners.

"Simplicity is the ultimate sophistication." *Leonardo da Vinci*

1. *Sit* down with family, friends, coworkers, peers, or whoever is around, and turn off all electronics.

2. *Sip* on tasty coffee and snack on your favorite treats.

3. *Smile* as much as you can, relax, and do your best to have an enjoyable, friendly, casual conversation.

After about 15 minutes, go back to your day feeling happy, energized and enthusiastic!

From Undoable to Done Overnight

On September 2, 1967 all of Sweden drove on the left side of the road, as they had always done. On September 3, 1967 the entire country awoke and suddenly had to drive on the right. In one single night, the entire country changed essentially everything they knew about driving.

A reasonable guess would be that it was a dark and bloody day for the country, with car parts flying every which way. But that guess would be totally off.

During the first Monday after the change, the amount of accidents actually fell below the average Monday accident rate, and for the next six weeks, accidents dropped 40 percent.

In truth, this is a just another excellent illustration of how powerful it is to have a society that is built upon a foundation of connection and caring. Everybody on the road had to be extra aware, they had to be conscious of the people around them and be ready to handle anything that might be thrown at them — and they pulled it off! Was this incredible societal success due entirely to Fika? Probably not. But it is definitely an indication of just how powerful it can be when an entire society adopts a compassionate and understanding view of itself, rather than a competitive and fearful one.

Despite the fact that Sweden's entire population is only 9.9 million (for comparison, in Los Angeles alone there are over 10 million people), Sweden somehow manages to stay at the forefront of business, design, science, sports, politics and social change on a global scale. And, Sweden is actually the #3 music producer in the world, behind only the USA and UK.

The Swedish Success Secret

To name a few of their most famous accomplishments, Sweden has given the world Volvo, Spotify, Skype, Zippers, Electrolux, Ultrasound, Ikea, H&M, ABBA, Zlatan Ibrahimovic, and so much more. Plus, and perhaps most significantly of all, a Swede invented the three-point seatbelt that we see in every car today — but he never patented the design, so it is free to use, and now this design is estimated to save a life every six minutes.

As if this level of achievement weren't enough, in Sweden, everybody gets five weeks of paid vacation per year, free education (yes, we mean college and post-grad, too), 16 months of paid parental leave and comprehensive healthcare that costs a maximum of roughly $130 per year. Some people hear this and think, "Oh that's just because they take everything in taxes!" But, in truth, the Swedish tax structure does not look all that different from California's...

Plus, Sweden has consistently ranked as a top-10 happiest country, the number one most equal country and the best country for women. Also, they have historically maintained a very immigration-positive policy and a neutral stance in major wars since 1814.

So does Fika work? Yes. Of course there are more factors at play, but Fika is no small part of that. Fika gives us the chance to truly connect on a societal level, and relearn what it means to truly care for each other. And the effects are clearly profound.

The Fika Attitude

In Fika, as in life, it's all about attitude. When we sit down to Fika, it's crucial to come with an attitude based in...

F*riendliness*

I*ntent*

K*indness*

A*wareness*

Friendliness

Unfortunately, a common way for people to make connections is through anger, gossip or complaining. Although these techniques might work for creating a momentary bond, relationships built upon this type of negativity are most often neither beneficial nor sustainable. But, by focusing on friendliness, we can ensure that our Fikas are always positive, rejuvenating and invigorating experiences for everybody who shows up, no matter how different or unfamiliar they might be — and that is absolutely crucial, especially today.

Intent

One simple question many people forget to ask themselves is "Why am I doing this?" When it comes to Fika, it's important to know why you're there and what you're trying to accomplish. If you come into Fika with the intention of creating a fun, communal experience then you probably will! But the opposite is true if you come in feeling angry, resistant or upset...

Kindness

Although this one should go without saying, we could all use a little more kindness in our lives. Rather than being right or superior, try to be understanding and compassionate at Fika — there's no quicker shortcut to connection than that.

Awareness

Many people go through life unaware of so much, from how they present themselves to how other people are feeling. When we make the choice to be aware of ourselves and the people around us, it's amazing how much easier it is to build connections and create the lives we crave.

And remember, the Fika attitude shouldn't stop just because Fika time is over. This is a major shortcut to unlocking the magic of Fika in all aspects of your life.

Fika Philosophy
Swedes Do It Several Times Per Day

The Fika philosophy revolves around the importance and tangible benefits of taking time, uninterrupted by technology or the outside world, to just connect with the people around you. Now, when almost 80 million Americans report having not even one close friend, it's more crucial than ever to create spaces for our communities to connect every day — if for no other reason than to help the millions of people who might be all alone in this world.

"One of the most important things you can do on this earth is to let people know they are not alone."
Shannon L. Adler

The magic of this tradition is that it not only values coffee and break time (like the all-too-common coffee grab'n'go,) but also emphasizes friendship and connection as something valuable and crucial, rather than secondary and inconvenient.

"We are social animals, and we have evolved to be in groups. We have always needed others for our survival. It's in our genes." *Professor Tasha R. Howe*

Fika is so important to Swedish culture and business because it gives people the opportunity to create and foster relationships that might otherwise fall by the wayside. When we feel like people actually care about us and what we do, we inevitably do better. So, Fika is not just a little coffee break, it's actually a proven tool for improving wellbeing, productivity, engagement and creativity within groups and organizations of all kinds.

But we've made it this far without Fika, why should we start today?

Today in the U.S.A. alone, almost *80 million* people report having not even one friend to talk to, and almost the same amount report being under "extreme stress." Coincidence? Almost certainly not.

Even though people are now more "connected" than ever – because of technology and social media – one doesn't have to look far to see how isolated we have become. Research shows that people now feel lonelier than ever before...

What came first, stress or loneliness?

Today, it seems like stress and loneliness are everywhere. And, unfortunately, the more stressed we get, the more we isolate ourselves. And the lonelier we get, the more stressed out we feel.

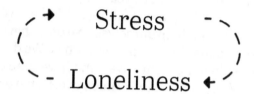

Our culture has entered into somewhat of a vicious cycle, wherein our collective levels of stress and loneliness just keep growing and growing, feeding off one-another. When we feel stressed, we enter into patterns of isolation. And when we feel isolated, we enter into patterns of stress. So the two feed on one-another and grow into something so overwhelming that we can't even address it.

"Stress is an ignorant state. It believes that everything is an emergency." *Natalie Goldberg*

As we grow more stressed and lonely, we imprison ourselves in a no talking zone, wherein the primary form of connection we share with one-another is through technology. One doesn't have to look far to see the results of this trend: people spend their breaks, free time and everything in between plugged into their phones, computers or TVs, yet have serious difficulty communicating with the people around them.

No Time for a Good Time

"One of the symptoms of an approaching nervous breakdown is the belief that one's work is terribly important." *Bertrand Russell*

These days so many of us hurry through life as if it were a race that we need to win by reaching the end first. We don't have time to help those falling behind or even stop to take a breath and help ourselves. We don't have time to spend with friends, family and loved ones. We don't have time to invest in our dreams. We don't have time to have a good time. We live in a state of time poverty, never feeling we have enough.

"Sleep faster! We need the pillow." *Sign in a Hotel*

On stress, we're like racehorses with blinders on. We quickly rush by everyone, unable to see anything but what's right in front of us. When we're stressed out, the last thing we want to do is sit down and actually talk to anybody — we actively avoid it. Instead, we text, email and hide behind our devices, and eventually, we start to avoiding talking to anybody at all. Even calling the people we care most about begins to feel like a chore when we are so overwhelmed by all of the "busy-ness" in our lives.

Most of us are getting busier and busier, but unhappier and unhappier. We are taught that "busyness" is a sign of success or importance, but we ignore our basic need for closeness and happiness. So often we feel we just don't have enough time or energy to invest in relationships, when we have so much else to do.

> **"Loneliness undermines peoples' ability to self-regulate... Is it any wonder that we turn to ice cream and other fatty food when we are sitting at home, feeling all alone in the world?"**
> *Dr. John Cacioppo*

Usually, after a long day, the need for some good feelings catches up with us, but, by then, we're too tired to do much about it. So, we often try to fill that void by searching for instant gratification in things like a glass of wine, mouthful of sweets, another episode of our favorite show, etc. But these things rarely help because they isolate us even further, helping that loneliness to grow, making us feel even worse and less interested in creating connection. It's a vicious cycle that millions, and more each day, are stuck in.

"The biggest disease today is not leprosy or tuberculosis, but rather the feeling of being unwanted, uncared for, and deserted by everybody."
Mother Teresa

Loneliness Is The New Smoking

Despite the fact that roughly 1/4 of Americans are chronically lonely, loneliness is often regarded as a personal problem. So we feel ashamed about it and keep it quiet. It's becoming clearer and clearer, though, that loneliness is a societal problem that affects us all in one way or another.

Studies show that loneliness is flat out dangerous: it causes high levels of stress and can lead to sleeping disorders, a weakened immune system and higher risk of both depression and suicide. Experts say loneliness is the new smoking because prolonged loneliness has been shown to be as bad for your health as smoking 15 cigarettes a day.

"Communication leads to community, that is, to understanding, intimacy and mutual valuing." *Rollo May*

Few things have a stronger impact on wellbeing than human connections. There is almost no better way to predict somebody's sense of happiness than by looking to the quality and quantity of their relationships. Several studies show that people who have good relationships with others tend to be healthier, happier and more successful.

Loneliness, on the other hand, often leads to depression, health issues and generally decreased feelings of wellbeing. One doesn't have to look far to see the real-world effects of this lonely, isolated, stressed out culture we live in...

Only 6 percent of Americans think the world is getting better

We are one of the most pessimistic countries in the world, with 57 percent of our population believing that our way of life will end in the next 100 years and 30 percent believing that our entire species will be extinct within that time.

The USA is not even in the top 15 happiest countries in the world

Despite being the most powerful and arguably most privileged country in the world, the USA is definitely nowhere near the happiest. How can that be?

Since the 1930s, young Americans have been reporting increasing levels of Anxiety and Depression each year.

"I think the research tells us that modern life is not good for mental health." *Dr. Jean Twenge, Author of Generation Me: Why Today's Young Americans Are More Confident, Assertive, Entitled—and More Miserable Than Ever Before*

40.5 million Americans use some form of psychiatric drug

In the last 30 years, antidepressant use in America has risen 400 percent — one in 10 adults now use some form of antidepressant.

Over 70 percent of Americans are unhappy in their current jobs.

In a society that places so much emphasis on what we "do" for a living, this statistic is quite terrifying. When unhappiness is the norm in any company, or society, productivity, loyalty and general wellbeing all start to sink, and we all inevitably suffer.

Almost 2/3 of Americans Don't Get Any Recognition at Work

When 2/3 of us are not receiving recognition at work, it's clear that there is a problem with isolation in this country. We don't feel like we can reach out to each other or that anybody wants to reach out to us. The #1 reason people leave their jobs is because they feel under-appreciated, and employees who quit their jobs can cost their company almost 150 percent of their salary to replace. But, when people feel engaged and invested in their companies, they are 87 percent more likely to stick around.

Unhappy workers cost the US economy over $550 billion per year

Studies have shown that happy employees are up to 20 percent more productive than their unhappy counterparts. But, "unhappiness" is so rampant that it currently costs almost 1/3 of the USA's GDP. So, it's clear that happiness is not just some lofty idea, it has very real consequences even in business.

Americans Devote more than 10 hours per day to screen time

"I fear the day that technology will surpass our human interaction. The world will have a generation of idiots."
Albert Einstein

Solitary confinement is one of the worst possible punishments for prisoners, and it is known to have severe, lasting mental repercussions. Still, many of us put ourselves in a form of solitary confinement everyday by choosing to isolate ourselves in front of our screens.

"Apparently we love our own cell phones but we hate everyone else's." *Joe Bob Briggs*

"**If you don't regularly exercise your ability to connect face-to-face, you'll eventually find yourself lacking some of the basic biological capacity to do so.**"

Dr. Barbara L. Fredrickson

But we don't have to be stuck in this stress and loneliness cycle...

FIKA THAT!

By incorporating connection, breaks and coffee into our daily lives we can effectively break the cycle of loneliness and stress that has a grip on so many of us. And it's as easy as just taking 15 minutes per day to take a break, chat with friends and enjoy some coffee!

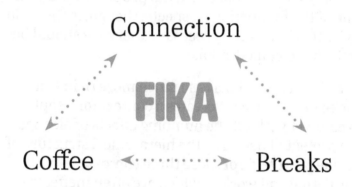

Now, more than ever, we need simple way to destress and connect with one-another. We need opportunities to meet people in a non-pretentious context that isn't dependent upon alcohol or lust. We need the support of our peers, friends and families to re-center our-selves and remember what is important in our lives.

"Happiness is a choice. You can choose to be happy. There's going to be stress in your life, but it's your choice whether you let it affect you or not."
Valerie Bertinelli

The Heart of Fika

At a very basic, boiled down level, Fika is about connecting, in person, over coffee and a snack. It's a 15
minute oasis, without work or technology, wherein
the only goal is to chat with the people around you.
One of the foundational aspects, though, is the inclu-
sivity that drives the process — everyone should be
actively welcomed at Fika.

The main reason Fika is so much more than just a
coffee break is that it creates a context for people
to connect without the numbing effects of alcohol,
the pretext of dating or the hierarchical structure of
business. Outside of those three contexts — party-
ing, dating and work — which are often ineffective
at creating lasting relationships, there are not many
institutions available to provide the daily dose of
connection that we all need. Fika provides a simple,
friendly, inclusive setting for people to break bread,
share some coffee and connect just for the sake of
connection; and the effects are profound.

**"The need for connection and commu-
nity is primal, as fundamental as the
need for air, water, and food."**
Dean Ornish

FIKA THAT!

The benefits of connection, in and of themselves, are enough to make Fika more than worth the time, but once you add in the benefits of breaks and coffee, it becomes almost too good to be true. The 15-minute Fika break has been shown to reduce stress levels and increase productivity, creativity and general wellbeing. Plus, the sharing of coffee and snacks establishes trust and connection in a way that is hard to describe. When we break bread with somebody, something happens that connects us on a primal, very human level. Add in the health and mental benefits of drinking coffee, and you have a recipe for 15 of the best, most worthwhile minutes of your day.

Section #2:

Coffee

"You can't buy happiness, but you can buy coffee, and that's pretty close."
Anonymous

Death by Coffee

Gustav III, the king of Sweden in the late 1700s, was very suspicious of coffee. In an attempt to scare people away from the drink and the conversations it could lead to, he thought up a cruel experiment:

To prove the deadly effects of the foul substance, twins convicted of murder were sentenced to death by coffee. One twin was forced to drink three pots of coffee per day and the other was given three pots of tea. Gustav's plan was to show how quickly the coffee would kill the first twin as compared to his identical tea-drinking brother. So Gustav ordered two doctors to oversee the experiment and tell him as soon as one of the twins died.

Unfortunately for Gustav III, before either of the twins succumbed to their punishment, both of the doctors died, and the king himself was assassinated. Finally, at the ripe old age of 83, the first of the twins died... It was the tea-drinker.

But, why coffee? What is the significance of basing this entire tradition around coffee? Isn't coffee actually bad for you?

The answer is quite simple, really. Coffee is the best! Okay, in all honesty, although that is true, that is not the only reason. Coffee is such a universal treat that it creates a common ground between people who otherwise might not realize they have anything in common at all. Most connections only need a little spark to get started, and coffee is the spark in the Fika concept.* Plus, it has an incredibly long history of inspiring great leaders, artists and revolutionaries...

Fika is the Context for Connection. Coffee is the Catalyst.

To help you understand why we, and so many people around the world, are so in love with coffee, we've put together a mini-history of coffee and all its magic. Enjoy!

*Fika is not truly dependent upon coffee, though. If you prefer tea, a smoothie, or even just water, that is totally fine. The traditional choice, and our choice, is coffee, but like all good traditions, Fika is constantly evolving and changing — so make it your own!

The Common Ground

"I was taken by the power that savoring a simple cup of coffee can have to connect people and create community."
Howard Schultz

Even through all the ebbs and flows of public opinion, coffee has remained one of the most universal, culturally significant products of all. Today, it is the second largest commodity in the world, second only to crude oil. In that way, few things unite humanity like coffee does. Every day, the world drinks more than 2.3 billion cups of coffee. Aside from essential biological functions, there is almost nothing that our species does more often or universally!

This love for coffee is nothing new, either. From the 16th to the 18th century, coffee's popularity sky-rocketed all across Europe. By the mid 18th century, there were over 600 coffee houses in Paris alone. Coffee, which had once been seen mainly as medicine, was now being looked at as a central part of the daily social scene.

Along with this meteoric rise of coffee houses across Europe came the rise of the age of reason and, with that, the age of rebellion. All of a sudden, people were having intelligent and meaningful conversations in public, without the numbing effects of alcohol. And this meant kings suddenly had to be concerned about the conversations that were taking place in coffee houses, as those could easily lead to rebellion... which they often did.

Strong Feelings About the Strong Brew

"Almost all my middle aged and elderly acquaintances, including me, feel about 25, unless we haven't had our coffee, in which case we feel 107." *Martha Beck*

Essentially, since its discovery 1000 years ago, people have consistently loved and hated coffee, rarely anything between. Sometimes it's been sold as a medicine, others it's been avoided like a poison. People have worshipped coffee, protested against it, killed for it and even feared it as the drink of the devil... That is until the pope blessed it.

In Constantinople, for example, coffeehouses were so highly regarded that they earned the name Qahveh Khaneh, which means Schools of Wisdom. And if a husband couldn't provide his wife with enough coffee, she had legal grounds for divorce.

Whereas in London in 1674, Women formed a group to protest coffee because their men were always at the coffee houses, and not at home as needed during domestic crises. Thus, the Women's Petition Against Coffee was born...

"Coffee leads men to trifle away their time, scald their chops, and spend their money, all for a little base, black, thick, nasty, bitter, stinking, nauseous puddle of water." *Women's Petition Against Coffee*

Coffee and War

On the opposite end of the spectrum, coffee has been a surprisingly significant factor in multiple wars and revolutions...

Benjamin Franklin was not just a legendary revolutionary, he was also an avid coffee drinker. When he was the ambassador to Sweden in 1782, he had so many Fikas with the Swedish leaders that he was able to convince them to become the second country in the world to recognize the United States' newly gained independence (the first was Britain, for obvious reasons.)

"Among the numerous luxuries of the table... coffee may be considered as one of the most valuable."
Benjamin Franklin

Later, during the American Civil War, the word "coffee" was used more often in the diaries of the Civil War soldiers than almost any other word, including "war," "slavery," "mother," and even "Lincoln." Coffee played such a big role in the war, in fact, that Sharps Rifle Co. began making a rifle with a coffee grinder built into the handle.

"If your men get their coffee early in the morning, you can hold." *General Benjamin Butler*

"We are reduced to quarter rations and no coffee... And nobody can soldier without coffee." *Ebenezer Nelson Gilpin*

On the opposite side of the globe, many years later, Sweden's access to coffee was cut off in the heat of WWII. In desperation, the Swedes developed a staggering 144 coffee substitutes. Despite the renowned creativity, ingenuity and scientific prowess of the Swedes, none of the coffee imposters did the trick.

Famous Coffee Lovers

In addition to being fuel for Fika, revolution, wisdom, conversation and war, coffee and coffee houses have been a source of inspiration for some of the greatest artists, writers, and musicians of all time...

"Without my morning coffee I'm just like a dried up piece of roast goat."
Johann Sebastian Bach

"Way too much coffee. But if it weren't for the coffee, I'd have no identifiable personality whatsoever."
David Letterman

"I have tried to show the café as a place where one can go mad."
Vincent Van Gogh

"The powers of a man's mind are directly proportioned to the quantity of coffee he drinks."
Sir James Mcintosh

"Coffee is a language in itself."
Jackie Chan

"Coffee is a lot more than just a drink; it's something happening... like an event, a place to be, but not like a location, but like somewhere within yourself."
Gertrude Stein

"Coffee is balm to the heart and spirit."
Verdi

"Behind every successful man is a surprised woman."
Maryon Pearson

**"Behind every successful woman is a
substantial amount of coffee."**
Stephanie Piro

From Coffee In A Sock
To the Melitta Coffee Filter

"The difficulty is not so much in developing new ideas as in escaping from old ones." *John Maynard Keynes*

Until the early 1900s, coffee filters were made of cloth, and sometimes people would even use their old socks. One day, Melitta Bentz decided she was tired of using socks to make her coffee, so she used a piece of paper from her son's homework and changed the coffee-brewing process forever.

"To invent, you need a good imagination and a pile of junk."
Thomas Edison

18 Ingenious & Effective Uses for Coffee Grounds

Repel Slugs and Other Pests
Fertilize Your Garden
Turbocharge Your Compost
Naturally Cleanse Your Hair
Exfoliate Your Skin
Clean Out the Fireplace
Treat Your Cellulite
Feed Your Worms
Absorb Food Odors
Deter Cats
Scour Your Pans
Clean and Deodorize Your Drains
Tenderize Your Meat
Make an Air Freshener
Remove Dark Circles from Under Your Eyes
Clean a Dirty Grill
Wash Your Hands
Erase Scratches from Your Furniture

"I like the serendipitous surprises of reality."
Lawrence Wright

Voltaire is rumored to have drank 50+ cups of coffee per day. When someone warned him that it's a slow working poison, he said,

"I believe it. I've been drinking it for 65 years and I'm not dead yet."

The Coffee Cure

Unfortunately, despite all of its accomplishments and awards, many people still look at coffee as a small guilty pleasure instead of a healing, tasty, life-enhancing miracle brew. That's not surprising, though! Every superstar gets slammed with rumors now and again, and coffee is no different. It doesn't take much more than a simple google search to find research that proves what most of us already know: coffee is extremely good for you! A recent study even showed that people who drink coffee live longer than those who do not. Is coffee the fountain of youth? That's not for us to say, but the research definitely seems to suggest it.

When consumed responsibly and in moderation, coffee has been shown to...

- Lower the risk of diabetes
- Increase metabolism and energy production
- Protect against liver disease
- Protect against Parkinson's disease
- Improve thyroid function
- Decrease chance of heart failure
- Lower possibility of dementia and Alzheimer's
- Protect against certain cancers
- Lower risk of death, in general

"It is inhumane, in my opinion, to force people who have a genuine medical need for coffee to wait in line behind people who apparently view it as some kind of recreational activity." *Dave Barry*

"We human beings are social beings. We come into the world as the result of others' actions. We survive here in dependence on others. Whether we like it or not, there is hardly a moment of our lives when we do not benefit from others' activities. For this reason, it is hardly surprising that most of our happiness arises in the context of our relationships with others."

Dalai Lama XIV

The Fika Revolution is Brewing

Coffee has been an active part of daily life across the world for thousands of years. Somewhere along the line, though, the social aspect of coffee started to fade, and it was replaced by the grab and go culture. Today, cafés and coffee breaks are filled with phones and computers rather than lively conversation.

But now, once again, the Fika Revolution is brewing. Around the world, people are starting to remember that coffee is much more than just a drink — it's a catalyst for connection. That is why Fika and coffee go hand in hand — Fika brings people together, and coffee unites them.

The universal love of coffee is the perfect common ground upon which we can build our love for each other. At the very least, we all speak the language of coffee, and maybe that's the perfect place to start seeing how we can all speak the language of friendship, too.

Section #3:

Breaks

"I'm trying not to put too much pressure on myself, but I think I'm overcompensating. I'm putting too much pressure on myself to not put too much pressure on myself."

Dan Billardello

The Leaky Bucket

There once was a woman who lived in a Rural Village. Each day, she walked five miles from her house to the well to get water for her family. This walk took up most of her day, as it was a 10-mile roundtrip journey. Still, the woman walked the whole way with a smile on her face, whistling and enjoying the scenery.

She walked with a bucket in each hand, but one of the buckets had a little crack in the bottom. By the time she got home each day, the cracked bucket only held half of the water that it did when she left the well.

After years of leaking, the cracked bucket said to the woman, "I fail you every day, I make your life more difficult and I lose water for your family. Please just destroy me and use my wood to make a new bucket, I do not wish to fail you any longer."

The woman smiled down at her leaky bucket, picked it up and hugged it with all her might. She said, "My dear, leaky bucket, without you my journey would be a very sad one. Where do you think all these flowers along my path came from? If you didn't water them, there would be no flowers for me to enjoy. Your leaking is the reason I have such beauty around me, the reason I smile and whistle every day. I wouldn't trade you for anything."

"We will be more successful in all our endeavors if we can let go of the habit of running all the time, and take little pauses to relax and re-center ourselves. And we'll also have a lot more joy in living."
Thich Nhat Hanh

Break out!

The Leaky Bucket story is an excellent example of how something that looks like a weakness or a flaw might actually be a thing of strength or beauty...

Although the bucket assumed its leak was ruining the woman's day by dripping water, it was in fact making her life much better and more beautiful. This idea is a perfect mirror for the Fika Break. Many people assume that taking breaks is lazy and wasteful because it is time spent "away from the important stuff." But, in truth, breaks — just like the leaky bucket — can motivate, energize and inspire us.

Breaks are so much more than just *time away* from something, they are actually a very important aspect of a successful, healthy and happy life. In fact, in Sweden, the Fika Break is widely considered to be one of the most imporant and productive times of the day.

"Science may never come up with a better office communication system than the coffee break."
Earl Wilson

Management by Fika

"'Police Work wouldn't be possible without coffee,' Wallander said. 'No work would be possible without coffee.' They pondered the importance of coffee in silence."
Henning Mankell

Fika is a central part of daily life in Sweden. Somehow, despite this tradition of taking breaks at least a couple of times a day to drink coffee and chat, Sweden is one of the most productive and innovative countries in the world. Or is that maybe why?

"Camaraderie is more than just having fun. It is also about creating a common sense of purpose and the mentality that we are in it together."
Christine Riordan, Harvard Business Review

Despite the fact that it takes place during a break, Fika is one of the Swedes' biggest and best secrets to success. Many managers say the 15 minutes spent on Fika are some of the best and most effective they spend all day. Surprisingly enough, there is research to suggest that breaks like Fika, and the results they produce, not only create better workplace environments, but can increase productivity tremendously — by up to 50 percent. Taking the time to actually talk to one-another helps us communicate more effectively and avoid drama, problems and useless distractions, and it just makes us feel better!

Breakthrough!

"Swedes are the masters of informal networking – they even invented a word for meeting up and talking over a cup of coffee: to "Fika." It's both a verb and a noun. Most of all, it's an incredible way to meet new people and exchange ideas." *Marco Ortolani*

Chances are that every day you use something the Swedes developed between Fika breaks: Spotify, Skype, GPS, seatbelts, zippers, at screen monitors, energy saving light bulbs...

"Progress isn't made by early risers. Its made by lazy men trying to find easy ways to do something."
Robert Heinlein

So, by taking a 15-minute break each day to have Fika and invest in your happiness and wellbeing, you're not being selfish — you're actually helping yourself be the best version of yourself that you can be!

"It's important to listen to everyone and through the communal nature of Fika, chatting between employees and management is encouraged. It's a great way to get everyone's view on how companies are run."
Andreas Åström, Stockholm Chamber of Commerce

The Fika Fix

"Social bonds that result from daily interactions among co-workers can lead to greater collaboration. Well-designed beverage areas in the workplace have actually been found to improve productivity." *Phyllis Korkki, NYT.com*

Fika is so important to Swedes that it's a fixture in every day's calendar — at home, in the workplace and with friends. Even though one might think that taking breaks like this all the time would make it harder to actually get things done, study after study has shown that strategic breaks like Fika can actually boost productivity enormously. Breaks help keep people happy, relaxed and engaged, and this means they are more efficient, enthusiastic and effective than their unhappy, stressed and bored peers. After all, 30 percent of workers waste at least 30 minutes per day on non-work related tasks, like checking Facebook or browsing the internet, usually out of boredom or exhaustion.

> **"I know what I am trying to escape, but not what I am searching for."**
> *Michel de Montaigne*

Could that be you surfing the web at work around 3:00?

When we work for hours on end without breaks, we start getting distracted by little things, like side conversations, Facebook, emails and texts. So, at the end of the day, we've lost a good chunk of time to these nonbeneficial, nonproductive breaks, when we could have just taken a 15-minute Fika to actually recharge. In some ways, it's like napping — if you take 30 one-minute naps throughout the day, you probably wouldn't feel more rested at all. Whereas, if you took one 15-minute nap, you would almost certainly feel more rested, focused and ready to go. By investing in Fika, you're not only investing in yourself, but in your business or community, too.

"Studies show that people who take a break from their work do not do less. It's actually the opposite... Efficiency at work can benefit from these kinds of get-togethers."
Viveka Adelsward

Many people think of breaks as being contrary to work, like moments to slack or waste time. But, in truth, breaks are a crucial part of finding success in everything we do. The brain needs breaks in order to function at its full capacity and, when we don't take them, research shows that we are much less efficient and effective and more prone to distraction and stress. So we actually lose time by skipping the breaks...

That's great for the Swedes, but I just don't have the time... I'm way too busy!

"It is not enough to be busy. So are the ants. The question is: What are we busy about?"
Henry David Thoreau

~~Do you have time to take a break?~~
Do you have time to not take a break?

Newton discovered gravity resting under a tree, Archimedes discovered his principle while taking a bath, and Da Vinci took naps all the time! Who says breaks aren't productive?

Many of us have a poverty complex when it comes to our time. We feel that we just never have enough, no matter how hard we try. Of course, some people do lead lifestyles that require 24/7 "busyness," but most of us really could free up plenty of extra time in our day with a few simple changes.

"Until you value yourself, you won't value your time. Until you value your time, you won't do anything with it."
M. Scott Peck

We get so busy just being busy — we spend hours in the library or the office, but for a good amount of that time we're not actually doing anything productive. It's so easy to get distracted by this, that or the other thing, and then you blink and another day is gone.

"The right time to relax and take a break is when you don't have time for it." *Sydney J. Harris*

But there's actually a rather simple solution to this problem. When you break your day up into manageable chunks of time, rather than an overarching glob of 24 hours, it's easier to be much more efficient. A few minutes of conscious effort spent on planning every day could dramatically increase almost everyone's efficiency. A great first step is to ask yourself the following questions…

Create Your Gameplan!

1. What are your top three concrete, priority actions for the day?

2. What are the next three concrete things you would like to get done, after your priority actions are complete?

3. What are some extra loose ends you could tie up after completing your six priority actions?

"75 percent of my life is spent wasting time. The other 25 percent isn't nearly as productive."
Jarod Kintz

After you've identified what needs to be done, set a reasonable, result-oriented goal for the completion of each action. To work on "the project" for an hour is not a good goal. Instead, frame it as, "I will finish writing four pages of the project in an hour." Result-oriented goals are more effective and help you work much more efficiently.

Once you have a general framework for your day and a result-oriented goal set for each action, make sure to schedule time for Fika as a reward, and then get going! Now you won't spend all that time trying to figure out what you need to do next because you'll have it all laid out right in front of you.

The Final Piece of the Puzzle:
THE POWER HOUR

Even when we work toward our goals and do our best to ensure we are working efficiently, it can be extremely challenging to avoid constantly being interrupted by our phones, Facebook, or chit chat, and that costs us much more time than we might think. An interruption of even a few moments can cost us up to 10 minutes of productive work because it takes us several minutes beyond the actual interruption to get our minds refocused on the project in front of us. When get in the flow and stay in the flow, it is infinitely easier to actually be productive.

"Time management is an oxymoron. Time is beyond our control, and the clock keeps ticking regardless of how we lead our lives. Priority management is the answer to maximizing the time we have." *John C. Maxwell*

Try This! Commit to 50 minutes of uninterrupted work, followed by 10 minutes of checking on all the "other" stuff, like email, Facebook or your texts.

By eliminating small, nonproductive and nonbeneficial distractions, and giving ourselves a goal-oriented plan for the day, we can easily make enough time for Fika — even if we feel like our days are already totally booked up.

BONUS: Research shows that a moderate level of distraction – like the sounds of a coffee house – can actually boost your creativity. If you can't make it to a coffee house, you can get the sound of coffee houses right on your phone. There are videos on youtube, apps and entire websites dedicated to giving you the feeling of being in a coffee house.

With these techniques, you can easily set yourself up for a more productive, efficient and happy life — and it costs you nothing! With just a few moments of planning and a little focus, you can have all the benefits of breaks, be even more effective than you are right now, and have plenty of time left over for Fika!

**"Do the best you can
until you know better.
Then, when you know
better, do better."**
Maya Angelou

Section #4:

Connection

"The greatest gift of life is friendship, and I have received it."
Hubert H. Humphrey

The Optimistic Old Man

An old, grey, tired man complained to his doctor that he was feeling terrible. The doctor examined him with a grim look on his face, gave the man his diagnosis and sent him on his way.

A few weeks later, the doctor met the same old man on the street, but he hardly recognized him. Instead of the hunched-over, beaten-down, old man, the doctor was now looking a youthful, radiant gentleman laughing his way down the street with a beautiful lady on his arm. The doctor asked the old man, "What happened to you, sir? You look fantastic!"

"I just followed your advice, Doc!" the old man said.

"What advice?!"

"Well, you said to be cheerful and get yourself a hot mama!" said the old man.

The doctor stumbled back in shock and said, "What?! No! I said to be careful, you've a got yourself a heart murmur!"

"Studies indicate that 'social capital' is one of the biggest predictors for health, happiness, and longevity. The problem: we often do not recognize the importance of social connection. Our culture values hard work, success, and wealth, so it's no surprise some of us do not set aside enough time for social ties when we think security lies in material things rather than other people."

Cecile Andrews in an interview with BeWell@Stanford

The Power of a Smile Shared With a Friend

At first glance, the story of the Optimistic Old Man is quite a funny joke, but it is actually quite a bit more than that. This old man is a perfect illustration of just how important it is to know when to listen to others, and when to shut them out and just listen inward.

"Everything we hear is an opinion, not a fact. Everything we see is a perspective, not the truth."
Marcus Aurelius

Today, we are all bombarded with prescriptions for a better life: buy a bigger house, get a faster car, earn more money and then your life will be all roses and sunshine. But, as many people are beginning to see, it just doesn't work. Nothing can replace friendship and human connection. So, just like the old man, we have to learn to listen in to ourselves and find what really works for us. And, for most people out there, including the old man, sometimes the best medicine is just a good friend... or a "hot mama."

"Evidence shows that having even weak social connections in a stressful situation is really good for your health and your ability to handle that situation."
Jane McGonigal

Connection?
There's (not) an app for that

In today's technology-dominated world, it's easy to forget why we even need human connection at all. When there's so much to see and like on Facebook, and so many "people" right at our finger tips, it can be tough to see why it's even worthwhile to actually go out and talk to people... Well, as inconvenient as it may be, technology simply cannot replace real human connection.

"Social connection is such a basic feature of human experience that when we are deprived of it, we suffer."
Leonard Mlodinow

Research has found that the number of real, human friends you have is one of the best predictors of how many years you will live. That's right, having more friends seems to actually help you live longer. As if living longer wasn't enough, the World Happiness Report shows that social connections are also the biggest controllable factor that determines one's sense of happiness — unfortunately, Facebook friends don't count. So, not only do connections help you live longer, they make sure you enjoy all those years you are lucky enough to have. How much better can it get?

"The business of business is relationships; the business of life is human connection." *Robin S. Sharma*

Even though most people would like to have these magical friends that extend our lives and make us feel better, there are so few opportunities on a daily basis to actually find these friends! There is a reason that 80 million Americans can't find a close friend. It can be incredibly difficult to find a situation wherein it's natural, acceptable and easy to make new friends. Most of the casual experiences are either tied in with work, drinking or dating — and, generally, none of those are great at creating truly lasting friendships.

"The most important single ingredient in the formula of success is knowing how to get along with people."
Theodore Roosevelt

That is why Fika has the potential to be a real game-changer for us, as a country. Not only does Fika itself allow people to connect and destress, it also promotes a cultural mindset that allows and encourages connection between people of all kinds. By having Fika, we can, as a society, re-learn how to have casual connections that are not marred by inebriation, fear or lust.

There is no better context for learning the art of informal communication and human connection than sharing coffee, snacks and conversation with your peers every day. And, today, there are few things more pressing than re-learning how to connect and empathize with other people in this world.

Take the First Sip!

Most people are interested in having more friends, living a better life and feeling happier, but at the same time, many of us are not ready to get up and create those things for ourselves. There is a major obstacle most of us have to overcome in our pursuit of our goals: our own fear. Fear comes in all shapes and sizes, and we all have our own reactions to it. Eventually, though, there comes a point where we all have to look our fears in the face and stand our ground.

As gamers know, to get to the next level, you have to overcome — you've got to beat the boss, slay dragons and outsmart monsters. Part of the game is finding the best path, meeting the good guys, defeating the bad guys and eventually finding the treasure, then moving onto the next level and doing it all over again. What fun is a game with no challenges? The same is pretty much true of life — every obstacle, every fear you overcome gives you more power and experience than you had before.

Successful people look at rejections, failures and mistakes like a body builder looks at bigger weights — they're an opportunity to improve and get stronger. So learn from them and keep moving forward!

"Man cannot discover new oceans unless he has the courage to lose sight of the shore." *Andre Gide*

Maybe your fear is what stops you from reaching out to someone who seems lonely — someone you could smile at, say hi to, or share a Fika with one afternoon. But, fear of rejection, being awkward or pushy stops you from trying.

Unleash Your Inner Viking

Over a thousand years ago, the Vikings were able to navigate the open seas with nothing but know-how, some "magic" crystals and sun compasses. Today, we navigate using a different kind of Viking invention, the GPS from Sweden. But that still doesn't help most of us find what we're looking for. To navigate through stress and obstacles in life, we all need to have a strong inner compass — we need to unleash our Inner Vikings.

To unleash your Inner Viking means having the courage to try new things even if it feels unnatural, step up when you're facing challenges, let go of the comfort of the familiar and explore new possibilities in all aspects of life. Unleashing your Inner Viking means having the strength and character to live a fearless life, stand up for what you think is right, and help others do the same.

"If your actions inspire others to dream more, learn more, do more and become more, you are a leader."
John Quincy Adams

It can be a real challenge to have the courage to stay true to our Inner Vikings when it often seems so much easier to just stay stuck or go with the flow. But now, more than ever, our world needs us all to step up and lead from a place of strength, integrity, courage and kindness to help one-another unleash our Inner Vikings and create a better world.

Be a Fika Leader

Unleashing your Inner Viking is not always an explosive process. It can be as simple as inviting a lonely coworker to Fika, taking an extra moment to pick up a piece of trash on the sidewalk, or smiling on the walk to work. Imagine if one person notices you going out of your way to make a difference, and they suddenly feel inspired to do the same, and that wave spreads throughout the world. What an enormous, world-changing difference a single moment of positivity and integrity can make...

"A leader is one who knows the way, goes the way, and shows the way." *John C. Maxwell*

And, even if nobody else notices your good deeds, there is always one person who does — you. Doing things that make you feel proud of yourself is how you build self-esteem and self-respect, and there are few things more valuable than that.

It's Easy as ABC

Even those of us who are immensely courageous need to have a direction for that courage to flow, and not everybody knows how to start connecting with others right off the bat. So we've created the coffee, caring & connection ABC to help you get started quickly and easily! Each letter in this alphabet has a unique coffee recipe to share with your Fika friends, and a tip for how to become the best connector that you can be.

We designed this section to be as interesting as a real Fika should be, with awesome ideas from some of the most inspirational people of all time and great drinks to go along with them. Though it may seem simple, this book is based on extensive research that we have packaged in tasty, little sips, so you can experience a more connected, happier life, starting today!

But, First... 3 major shortcuts!

1. Humorology 101

One of the quickest, most effective and least difficult ways to connect with somebody is through humor. A smile, laugh or a good joke transcends our minds and connects us at a level that almost nothing else can. That's why humor is such an important factor in Fika.

Today, adults laugh 15 times per day, on average. When compared to the average child who laughs 300-500 times per day, adults suddenly seem incredibly serious. If we were as forgiving as children, and could live in the moment and laugh at everything like they do, we might also have that boundless joy and energy of theirs. We need ways to practice smiling and laughing because these are incredibly important skills that actually affect our bodies, as well as our minds.

Studies have shown that smiling can actually make you happy, not just the other way around. It sounds crazy, but with each smile — whether we cause it ourselves or something else does — our bodies relax, release endorphins, get a mood and immune system boost and experience a drop in blood pressure. Plus, smiling is actually contagious. We instinctively smile when we see somebody smile at us. So, in a way, smiling is... well, no joke!

"A serious and good philosophical work could be written consisting entirely of jokes." *Ludwig Wittgenstein*

Humor can give us new perspectives, take the edge off of a tense situation, turn a conversation in a new direction, help us lift above our less desirable thoughts, allow us to relax and even help us create a sense of intimacy. A smile is the shortest distance between two people, and shared laughter creates a bond faster than almost anything else. So, it's incredibly important to give ourselves time to practice every day because some of us are not very good at laughing or smiling, and those people need our help!

Laughing and smiling are two of the most important and most beneficial parts of Fika because we could all use a little break from the stresses and troubles we have to deal with. So, by coming to Fika ready to give and create smiles and laughter, we can help one-another relearn how to go through the day with a sense of humor, rather than dread. And, in the process we can build stronger, more beneficial and closer connections with less stress and more fun.

"Let us be grateful to the people who make us happy; they are the charming gardeners who make our souls blossom." *Marcel Proust*

When you sit down to Fika, it's a good idea to come with some good news, funny stories or interesting topics for conversation. Fika is not the time to argue, criticize or make fun of people, it's an opportunity to practice creating connection through shared laughter, humor, joy and happiness. A successful Fika is one that you leave feeling better than you did when you walked in.

2. Put down the technology!

One of the ultimate shortcuts to creating more positive, enjoyable, rewarding connections in your life is so simple that it just might seem crazy — turn off your tech!

If human connection is what you want, you cannot expect technology to create it for you. We have to allow ourselves to be present with one-another in person and hear the voices, feel the warmth and share in the presence of the people around us.

Some people walk around with earbuds in 24/7 and wonder why nobody talks to them or why they just can't seem to make friends. By choosing to listen to the sounds of another place and time, we essentially reject the time and place we're in and everybody in it — we put up our very own "quiet please" sign and effectively remove ourselves from right here and now..

Take the risk of turning off the cellphone. What do you have to lose? Maybe you'll be bored for a few minutes as you sit on the subway, but what's so terrible about that? Most people are bored when they're staring at their cellphones, anyway. The difference is that we have a real chance on getting a return on our investment when we invest in the reality of life around us. When we invest in technology, we have a real chance of missing out on that reality.

"The great myth of our times is that technology is communication." *Libby Larsen*

Try the Digital Detox

The challenge:
Go one week without...

1. Using any type of technology in public (excluding the tech you have to use for work)

2. Texting somebody instead of calling them

3. Checking any social media

After one week, you will be amazed at how much extra time, energy and confidence you miraculously have lying around. We're all human — it's good to remember that, sometimes.

3. Say "Hi!"

The simple act of saying "hi" is so much bigger than those two letters. That first, tiny step toward establishing a connection can make all the difference. Sometimes, you just have to go for it and be the one to step up and take charge. If you are tired of being ignored when you walk into a room, greet everybody else when you walk in — they won't be able to ignore you, then!

So many of us wait our whole lives for good fortune and happiness to land in our laps when often we could have gone out and created it for ourselves years and years ago. Saying "hi" is not just a way to make friends, it's a way to acknowledge your own power and ability to shape the world around you — you have the power to make someone's day with that "hi!" You have the power to create the life you need. You just have to choose to try something, see how it goes and build from there.

Don't let your imagined consequences stop you from getting out and doing something amazing. Maybe you'll fail the first, second and even 50th time around. But, first of all, what's so bad about failure? It's a fantastic tool to learn from! And second, maybe on that 50th try, you'll strike gold and instantly forget about the stumbles before then. You just have to be the one to take charge and put out an effort! That's the basis for connection, and the basis for a successful, happy life.

"You have to come to your closed doors before you get to your open doors... What if you knew you had to go through 32 closed doors before you got to your open door? Well, then you'd come to closed door number eight and you'd think, 'Great, I got another one out of the way'... Keep moving forward." *Joel Osteen*

"I used to feel so alone in the city. All those gazillions of people and then me, on the outside. Because how do you meet a new person? I was very stumped by this for many years. And then I realized, you just say, 'Hi.' They may ignore you. Or you may marry them. And that possibility is worth that one word."

Augusten Burroughs

Section #5:

ABCs of Coffee, Caring & Connection

"A cup of coffee shared with a friend is happiness tasted and time well spent."
Anonymous

The Daring Dachshund & The Hungry Leopard

One day, a dachshund was on vacation with his owners in the jungle and he decided to go off a stroll on his own. After happily scampering along for a bit and taking in the sights, the dachshund noticed a leopard looking down from the trees. Having never seen anything like a Dachshund before, the Leopard watched suspiciously from the trees above.

Realizing the serious danger that he was in, the Dachshund quickly looked around for a way out, but the only thing in sight was a big pile of bones. Suddenly, he had an idea. As the leopard peered down from the trees, the Dachshund sat down on the bones, licked his lips and barked, "That was one tasty leopard! I wonder if there are any more around here..."

The Leopard heard the dachshund and froze mid-pounce. With fear in his eyes, the leopard ran back into the jungle as fast as he could. "Phew! That tricky little creature almost had me," he said. But a Monkey who was watching from the trees knew the Dachshund had tricked the Leopard. So the Monkey set off to tell the Leopard, hoping to get on the ferocious feline's good side.

Sure enough, the Leopard was furious! He roared and said, "You hop on my back and see what happens when creatures try to make a fool out of me!" So the monkey and the leopard set off to finish off that pesky Dachshund once and for all.

Little did they know, the quick little Dachshund had seen the monkey run off and figured that he was up to no good. So, just as the Dachshund heard the Leopard come crashing through the underbrush, he started gnawing on a bone and said, "Where is that useless monkey? I sent him to bring me another leopard hours ago!"

"All our dreams can come true, if we have the courage to pursue them."

Walt Disney

We chose to use the dachshund story right at the beginning of the ABCs because we think it is such a perfect example of the power that we each have to create change around us. Many of us are taught to settle for lives that don't really work for us, or just hope for a better tomorrow, but that little dachshund reminds us that we all have the opportunity to create a better life and world, right here and right now. We love that dachshund because he reminds us that, even when things seem at their worst, we can look life in the eyes, say "Fika That!" and make a change. With a little courage, a few friends and lots of coffee, anything is possible...

Americano

Equal parts espresso and hot water. It is said that the Americano was first brewed by American GIs in Italy during WWII. The soldiers would dilute espresso with water to make it taste more like the coffee they knew back home, so the Americano was born!

"I, not events, have the power to make me happy or unhappy today. I can choose which it shall be. Yesterday is dead, tomorrow hasn't arrived yet. I have just one day, today, and I'm going to be happy in it." *Groucho Marx*

Adopt an Amazing Attitude

"Attitude is a little thing that makes a big difference."
Winston Churchill

Lots of us get stuck in the habit of choosing the same, old, comfortable, worn-out attitude we've always put on, even though it might not actually fit anymore. We tend to view the same things in the same ways, day after day because we rarely take the time to stop and ask ourselves some simple questions: Why does this make me feel this way? Why do I choose to act this way? Why do I like this, and not that?

When we don't take the time to reflect on our attitudes, and make the effort to optimize them, we end up operating out of habit. And a very easy habit to develop is one of being critical, judgmental and resentful, rather than positive, enthusiastic and energetic. But when we get lost in our criticism, fear, anger or sadness, it becomes near impossible to truly appreciate what is actually in front of us – and life starts to seem a lot heavier, lonelier and less colorful.

One of the first steps in creating your Fika lifestyle is to experiment with changing your attitudes about the small, everyday things — like sitting in traffic, waiting in line, or dealing with your coworkers. Look for the magic, the beauty, the fun and the joy. Even this simple change can make a huge difference in your life.

"The greatest discovery of my generation is that a human being can alter his life by altering his attitudes."
William James

Bicerin

Two shots of espresso, one shot of drinking chocolate and two shots of whole milk. Mix the hot espresso and drinking chocolate together, add whole milk and mix it all up. This drink is a native of Turin, Italy and has been served there since the 18th century.

"Do Lipton employees take coffee breaks?" *Steven Wright*

Break Free!

What holds you back from creating the life you want? What fears, ideas, relationships or habits do you let slow you down?

"If we only wanted to be happy, it would be easy; but we want to be happier than other people, and that is almost always difficult, since we think them happier than they are." *Charles de Montesquieu*

We all have our ideas about what "normal" looks like, in terms of what is possible for us, how we should live our lives and who we should live them with. But, if we took a good hard look at what we consider normal, we wouldn't find it so normal at all. Is it really normal to spend 10+ hours per day glued to our screens, like Americans do? Is it really normal to overeat and overdrink to sate our desire for connection?

"The only normal people are the ones you don't know very well." *Alfred Adler*

It's time we break free from some of our assumptions about what normal life looks like, and create a lifestyle that is even better than normal — one that is extraordinary. Each day is an opportunity to create a better tomorrow! Whether it's just saying hi to five more people today, or inviting a friend to Fika this evening, it all starts with taking the first step, and having the courage to break free from the limitations we all put on ourselves.

"Of all the words of mice and men, the saddest are, "It might have been." *Kurt Vonnegut*

Cappuccino

The best cappuccino is made in equal parts: one part espresso, one part steamed milk and one part foamed milk. This drink earned its name because its unique color is very similar to the color of the robes that the Capuchin monks traditionally wear.

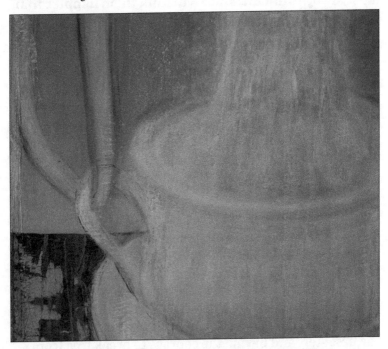

"The simple act of sitting here sipping this cappuccino is its own testament to my commitment to living the writer's life. Which is to say: doing nothing but doing it exceedingly well." *Sol Luckman*

Create!

"Creativity is piercing the mundane to find the marvelous."
Bill Moyers

Many of us get stuck in the "ugh" rut: Ugh! More work... Ugh! So much traffic... Ugh! What a long line. And unfortunately, when we're stuck down there, it can be almost impossible to get ourselves out. One of the keys to keeping yourself out of that ugh rut is to approach each day with a sense of creativity — to constantly be on the lookout for new ways of doing things, fun alternatives to boring tasks and interesting spins on old ideas. We each have the power to influence the world around us, but that doesn't just happen by accident. We have to put forth the energy of creativity and enthusiasm in order to effect change, even if that change is only within ourselves.

The creative eye is one that sees not only what is, but also what could be. The difference between a critical person and creative person, though, is that the critical person judges something as less good, whereas the creative person sees how to make it better. A creative life is a solution-oriented life!

"We can't do everything at once, but we can do something at once." *Calvin Coolidge*

One of the first solutions you can try to find right now is how to create a Fika tradition for yourself and your friends. Where would it be doable? How can you make it something that people would love to come to? What would be a good time to start this tradition?

"There is no innovation and creativity without failure. Period." *Brene Brown*

Down-Under Iced Coffee

Blend one cup of chilled coffee, one scoop of vanilla ice cream, one tsp of maple syrup and lots of ice. Once the drink has reached a smooth consistency, top with whipped cream and chocolate shavings. This is a classic Australian take on the regular ol' iced coffee.

"Decaffeinated coffee is kind of like kissing your sister."
Bob Irwin

Dare to Do It!

Many of us talk about the importance of loving, caring and connecting, but when it comes to practicing it in our daily lives we often have great excuses why we can't — we don't have the time, we're so tired, there's so much going on. So, instead, we sit, wait and hope for others to love us, care for us and connect with us. There is a major flaw in this tactic, though. What if everybody is just as busy, tired and otherwise occupied, too? Somebody has to be bold and take the first step! Why not you?

"You can't stay in your corner of the forest waiting for other to come to you. You have to go to them sometimes."
Winnie the Pooh

Sometimes we let other people – and ourselves – stop us from doing what we really want to do. We get so paranoid about failing, being judged or making a mistake that we've lost in our own minds before we've even tried to win. Sometimes you just have to get out there and do it, anyway!

"You miss 100 percent of the shots you don't take."
Wayne Gretzky

We all have that inner voice telling us to slow down, be careful and just take it easy — which is good advice every now again — but we also have to be ready to silence that hesitant, comfort-driven voice so that we can pounce when the moment comes. We have to be ready to jump into action and escape from our comfort zones when the opportunity presents itself.

"I'd rather regret the things I've done than regret the things I haven't done." *Lucille Ball*

Espresso

Espresso (not eXpresso) is strong coffee that is made by forcing steam through finely ground, roasted coffee beans – surprisingly enough, these are the same beans you find in regular coffee. A good shot of espresso will have a layer of golden-brown crema on top. One espresso shot has about 1/3 the caffeine of a regular cup of coffee.

Shared joy is double joy, shared sorrow is half sorrow.

Swedish Proverb

Exercise Empathy!

"Remember that everyone you meet is afraid of something, loves something and has lost something."
H. Jackson Brown

Many of us are brought up to look at the world as "them" and "us," and there is little room for compassion or empathy for those who are different. Even those who are similar to us are often seen as competitors, who we cannot afford to cooperate with or feel empathy for. In trying to create relationships, though, we have to set aside our competitive habits and relearn how to actually relate.

"Peace cannot be kept by force; it can only be achieved by understanding." *Albert Einstein*

When we open ourselves up to seeing things from perspectives other than our own and empathizing with them, it becomes much easier to gain a level of understanding for others. Instead of defending yourself or your perspective, try to really listen to someone who has an opinion that is totally different from yours, and try to find some common ground. Make an effort to be more understanding of the world, and you might find that the world starts to be more understanding of you.

Empathy can be a little tough to grasp as an abstract concept, so we've included a couple quotes from some inspirational people to give more insight into how we can all practice empathy more effectively...

"Empathy is the only human superpower — it can shrink distance, cut through social and power hierarchies, transcend differences, and provoke political and social change." *Elizabeth Thomas*

"When you show deep empathy toward others, their defensive energy goes down, and positive energy replaces it. That's when you can get more creative in solving problems." *Stephen Covey*

"Whenever you are about to find fault with someone, ask yourself the following question: What fault of mine most nearly resembles the one I am about to criticize?" *Marcus Aurelius*

"Empathy is a tool for building people into groups, for allowing us to function as more than self-obsessed individuals." *Neil Gaiman*

"I believe empathy is the most essential quality of civilization." *Roger Ebert*

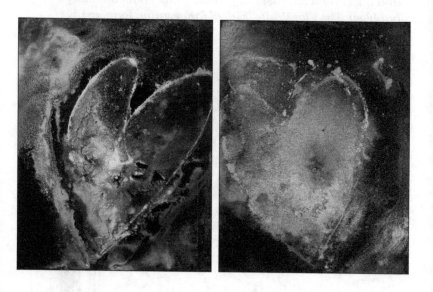

"Empathy is about finding echoes of another person in yourself." *Mohsin Hamid*

Flat White

Two shots of espresso topped with microfoam. The difference between this and a cappuccino is that the flat white uses microfoam (uniformly gooey steamed milk with tiny bubbles) and the cappuccino uses dry foam (foamy milk with large bubbles). The Flat White is ideal for creating foam art.

"Don't let fear or insecurity stop you from trying new things. Believe in yourself. Do what you love. And most importantly, be kind to others, even if you don't like them."
Stacy London

Fika That!

Some people are ready to jump straight into having epic Fika parties, and that's great! But for the rest of us who maybe want a little more step-by-step guidance, here are some major tips and shortcuts to creating the ideal Fika party.

Prepare Yourself for Fika!

"Everyone thinks of changing the world, but no one thinks of changing himself." *Leo Tolstoy*

---

1. Disinfect Yourself

Before you sit down and Fika with anybody it's important to wash your hands, both literally and metaphorically. Just like bacteria and viruses, the emotions we carry are infectious — for better or for worse. Make sure to wash off any negativity, gossip or criticism before you Fika so that the only infectious thing you bring to the table is your smile.

"Smiling is infectious; you can catch it like the flu. Someone smiled at me today, and I started smiling too." *Anonymous*

2. Location, Location, Location

Location and atmosphere are crucial to Fika! Try to pick a spot where there's enough room for everybody around the same table and it's not prohibitively loud. From there, it's important to make it feel festive with little things, like nice napkins, fresh flowers, beautiful baked goods, etc. Fika doesn't depend on fanciness, it just works best in a welcoming, comfortable and warm environment.

"My mom's funny that way, celebrating special occasions with blue food. I think it's her way of saying anything is possible. Percy can pass seventh grade. Waffles can be blue. Little miracles like that." *Rick Riordan*

3. Listen Up!

Word vomit is a real sickness and many of us suffer from it. We think that we need to fill every little silence with some sound, so we just keep talking. Just try to keep a few general rules in mind when having a casual conversation: Don't get too specific — let people ask for details. Complaining is a big turn off. Make space for the others in your conversation — it's not a competition, you're all on the same team. And, finally, practice active listening!

"I want to spend less time talking about myself, and more time listening to what other people have to say about me." *Jarod Kintz*

4. Don't Be Boring

For Fika to be at its best, everyone who comes should have the focus of giving others a good time, not just getting a good time from them. We can't expect other people to entertain us all the time, so it's important to put ourselves out there and crack a joke, tell a story or add some kindling to the conversation. Many people feel nervous to participate in conversation, but it is often much less enjoyable to sit across from a totally silent person than a totally ridiculous one.

"It's better to be absolutely ridiculous than absolutely boring." *Marilyn Monroe*

Be generous with your reactions. Smile, laugh, encourage and participate. Enthusiasm looks great on everybody. Try it and see how people suddenly enjoy your company much more.

Galao

Two shots of espresso, three shots of hot milk and sugar to taste. For maximum fanciness, serve this Portuguese staple in a tall glass.

"As we express our gratitude, we must never forget that the highest appreciation is not to utter words, but to live by them." *John F. Kennedy*

Go for Gratitude!

"Which one of these is the non-smoking lifeboat?"
Anonymous

If you're looking for the quickest way to a healthier, happier, wealthier and more fulfilled life, look no further! It's gratitude! Research has shown that focusing on gratitude for as little as five minutes per day can have the same positive effect on your happiness as doubling your income. Doubling it! Can you imagine that? If someone said to you, you can double your income in five minutes per day without even getting out of bed, you would jump for joy.

"Gratitude is the healthiest of all human emotions. The more you express gratitude for what you have, the more likely you will have even more to express gratitude for."
Zig Ziglar

Gratitude is also one of the quickest, simplest shortcuts to connection. Who doesn't like being thanked? There are few things more universally loved and accepted than appreciation — and it doesn't have to be for big, life-changing things. You can make somebody's day by thanking them for packing your bags at the grocery store. A simple *Thank You*! Costs nothing, but can pay off in huge ways. Even these little moments of kindness can be enough to carry somebody through their entire day, and you through yours.

"There's always something to be grateful for. If you can't pay your bills, you can be thankful you're not one of your creditors." *Anonymous*

Hot Coffee Masala

One cup of coffee, ¼ cup of milk, two cumin seeds, one whole star anise pod, one tsp cinnamon and two tsp sugar. In scalding hot coffee, mix all ingredients except milk. Remove seeds and pod after 3-4 minutes. Add hot milk. Enjoy!

"Whether you live to be 50 or 100 makes no difference, if you made no difference in the world." *Jarod Kintz*

Help out!

"Noble deeds and hot baths are the best cures for depression." *Dudey Smith*

Our society is so focused on what we want to have and own, that we often forget to consider what we want to share or give! It's a bit ironic because one of the quickest ways to build a happier, more successful life is to give, give and give some more. Still, many of us get so lost in trying to make our own lives work, that we don't even think about how we can improve the lives of the people around us – often, though, as we work to improve the lives of others, our own lives seem to magically become, well, magical.

"It is literally true that you can succeed best and quickest by helping others to succeed." *Napoleon Hill*

Start with something small: give a friend a few extra minutes of your time, instead of rushing off. Give someone a little extra attention if you see they aren't feeling great, or ask a neighbor if you could be of any help. But, as important as it is to help, it's also important to know when to take your hands off somebody else's wheel – everybody has to make their own mistakes.

"A kind man helps the fallen elephant. A stupid man tries to stop the elephant from falling." *Thai Proverb*

Instant Coffee

Many coffee snobs look down their noses at instant coffee, but there are some seriously delicious ways to make instant coffee, and it can save you some time and money. An easy way to avoid the watery taste that so many people associate with instant coffee is to just double up the recommended serving size in each cup. Top a strong cup of instant coffee off with some frothed milk and you'll have a better tasting cup of coffee than many people can make with even the fanciest equipment.

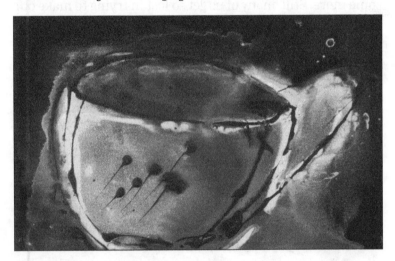

"What does it mean to be a superhero? We're all fighting for the better good. But, at the same time, I think what stands out is, as superheroes, you don't give up; you don't surrender. I think that's what makes a superhero."
Ellen Wong

Illuminate the way!

Many people go through life thinking that what they do and how they act doesn't really matter. But what if you suddenly found out that you were the ultimate role model for hundreds of people? What about thousands, or millions, even? Whether you know it or not, each one of us shapes the world around us with each choice and action. So, why not choose to be someone who illuminates the path toward a better world?

"Each time a man stands up for an ideal, or acts to improve the lot of others, or strikes out against injustice, he sends forth a tiny ripple of hope, and crossing each other from a million different centers of energy and daring, those ripples build a current that can sweep down the mightiest walls of oppression and resistance." *Robert Kennedy*

If you don't believe you actually have that power, consider this. Maybe one day as you walk down the street, you see a piece of trash. At that moment, you have the choice to pick it up or ignore it. Whether you recognize it or not, your decision will be noticed by at least a few people on that street with you. What if just one other person is inspired by your choice to pick up that piece of trash, and chooses to pick up the next piece of trash, themselves? Then, that choice inspires somebody else, and on and on. Imagine how many people — strangers, even — might be inspired to make a positive choice just because you did. Now, imagine if we weren't talking about picking up trash, but were talking about spreading joy, or acting with compassion, or something of that magnitude. The same concept applies!

Just Ice

Freeze coffee into cube form, blend with room temperature coffee and enjoy a chilled, non-watery iced coffee.

"Don't laugh at coffee. Someday you, too, might be old and weak." *Anonymous*

Just Joke!

"When she started to play, Steinway came down personally and rubbed his name off the piano." *Bob Hope*

It can be so easy to get upset, outraged, disgusted, etc. at so many things in life, and that's okay, but it rarely makes you feel better or improves the situation at all. Unfortunately, many of us just cruise through life in black and white, always allowing dark clouds to hover over us and our relationships, rather than stop and think: "What's the best way to enjoy this life?" Well, a very simple answer to that question is to simply look for the humor in everything. Nothing in this life is so sacred that it can't be improved with a smile and a laugh.

"After god created the world, he made man and woman. Then, to keep the whole thing from collapsing, he invented humor." *Guillermo Mordillo*

Try to celebrate the small, everyday moments, and put some fun into your life and the lives of the people around you! Serve your Fikas with a joke, or even just a beautiful flower or nice candle. If somebody tries to turn your day negative, try to turn the situation lighter with a joke, instead of reacting with rage or sadness. It's easy to have humor when everything is going smooth as butter, but during the times when it really counts – when it all hits the fan – it is much, much harder to remember to smile instead of scream, but it is also much, much more important.

"Despite the cost of living, have you noticed how popular it remains?" *Anonymous*

Laugh More!

"The early bird may get the worm, but the second mouse gets the cheese." *Anonymous*

Research shows that we laugh a lot less now than just 30 years ago, and the negative impact that has on our happiness, health and stress levels is immense.

"You grow up the day you have your first real laugh at yourself." *Ethyl Barrymore*

but...

"It's hard to enjoy practical jokes when your whole life feels like one." *Rick Riordan*

Just remember, if it will be funny to tell someone in a few years – it's funny now!

"Comedy is tragedy plus time." *Carol Brunette*

When we look at life through the lens of humor we start to see the world differently...

"From here to there, funny things are everywhere!"
Dr. Seuss

Too Much?
"Opera is when a guy gets stabbed in the back and, instead of bleeding, he sings." *Robert Benchley*

Too Late?
"I never drink coffee at lunch. I find it keeps me awake for the afternoon." *Ronald Reagan*

Too Hot?
"Go to Heaven for the climate and Hell for the company."
Benjamin Franklin Wade

Too Hungry?
"Ask not what you can do for your country. Ask what's for lunch." *Orson Wells*

Too True?
"In politics, stupidity is not a handicap." *Napoleon Bonaparte*

Too Distracting?
"A girl in a bikini is like having a loaded pistol on your coffee table – there's nothing wrong with it, but it's hard to stop thinking about it." *Garrison Keiller*

Too Long?
"'Oh jeez, there goes my ex-girlfriend. You know she started drinking when we broke up, and she never stopped.' 'Wow, I wonder how anybody can celebrate that long…'" *Anonymous*

Too Weak?
"If this is coffee, then please bring me some tea. If this is tea, please bring me some coffee." *Abraham Lincoln*

Kopi Luwak

Chances are you will never get to try this coffee – and you might not want to! It's some of the most expensive coffee in the world, sometimes priced at $1500 / lb and it comes from the digestive tract of an Asian Palm Civet (cat-like creature). They eat the berry and poop out the bean, supposedly tastier than it went in.

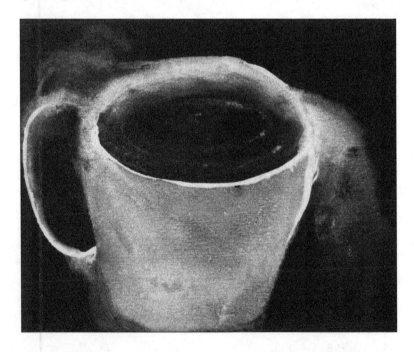

"You cannot do a kindness too soon, for you never know how soon it will be too late." *Ralph Waldo Emerson*

Keep it Kind!

"Since you cannot do good to all, you are to pay special attention to those who, by the accidents of time, or place, or circumstances, are brought into closer connection with you." *Saint Augustine*

Kindness is often put up on a pedestal reserved for only the grandest of gestures, but everyday kindness is usually the most important and rewarding. And it's so easy! Little acts of kindness — like buying the person behind you a cup of coffee, or bringing cookies for your Fika group — are proven to make everyone involved (the giver, receiver and observer) feel better because our brains release endorphins as we give, receive or observe kindness. So, by making others feel better, you are making yourself feel better, too.

"No act of kindness is too small. The gift of kindness may start as a small ripple that, over time, can turn into a tidal wave, affecting the lives of many." *Kevin Heath*

When you start looking for ways to be kind, you'll find there are opportunities at every turn: buy your coworker a coffee, invite someone to Fika, take out your neighbors' trashcans, visit an old relative or just send an email to someone who could use a little cheering up... At the very least, it's more fun than walking around preoccupied with your own problems all the time.

"A person who is nice to you, but rude to the waiter, is not a nice person." *Dave Barry*

Latte

One shot of espresso, two shots of steamed milk, and a layer of foamed milk on top. The Latte as we know it is an American creation, claimed by a coffee shop owner in Berkeley, CA. In Italian, "latte" literally means "milk." So ordering a latte in Italy will probably get you just what you asked for — a glass of milk.

"Most of the successful people I've known are the ones who do more listening than talking." *Bernard M. Baruch*

Listen Up!

Most people really appreciate someone who can listen, instead of just talking about themselves. So when we want to connect with people, we really do not need to be extraordinarily witty or charming, we just need to be great at listening and making people feel interesting.

"But enough about me. Let's talk about you. What do you think of me?" *Bette Midler*

Paying attention and actually listening to what's going on around you can be an extremely rewarding pursuit. Most successful leaders list being a good listener as one of their top strengths, and there is no better way to become good at listening than having Fika. The entire concept of Fika is centered around the practice of being present in conversation. When conversation is your main source of entertainment, even for 15 minutes a day, you learn how to listen and respond to people in a way that is becoming more and more rare — and more and more valuable.

"I didn't list listening as one of my skills. Probably because I didn't hear what the interviewer asked." *Jarod Kintz*

Still, sometimes we are so busy firing off our mouths, so eager to be heard that we forget to listen! It's amazing how willing most of us are to ramble on about things that we know so little about, when we could learn so much and make so many more friends, just by making an effort to actually listen to other people.

Mocha

Add a shot of espresso to your favorite hot chocolate. Coffee + Chocolate = Mocha. Back in the day, though, Mocha was just another name for coffee.

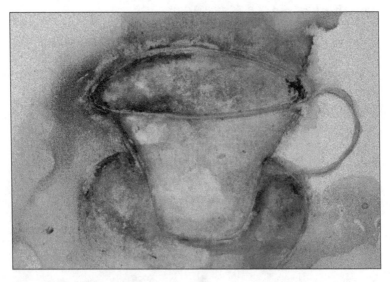

"Last comes the beverage of the orient shore, Mocha. Far off the fragrant berries bore, taste the dark fluid with a dainty lip. Digestion waits on pleasure as you sip."
Pope Leo XII

Make Your Own Luck

"I'm a great believer in luck and I find the harder I work, the more I have of it." *Thomas Jefferson*

Many people look at success as an impenetrable vault filled with treasure, and they just don't have the keys to get in. While other 'lucky' people seem to get in effortlessly. But research shows that being lucky is no accident. Only 10 percent of luck is determined by chance. The other 90 percent is in your own hands. You create your own luck! And, just like any skill, being lucky takes effort and practice.

"Luck is not a magical ability or gift from the gods... Instead, it is a way of thinking and behaving."
Richard Wiseman

Habits like building good relationships, smiling, having a positive attitude and looking for the opportunity in every situation are proven to be some of the biggest factors in creating luck. So, really, Fika is an excellent opportunity to practice being lucky.

"Success is simply a matter of luck. Ask any failure."
Earl Wilson

Want to be luckier?

"You gotta try your luck at least once a day, because you could be going around lucky all day and not even know it."
Jimmy Dean

---

1. Pay attention to and capitalize on opportunities as they present themselves.

Many people wait for luck to come knocking on their door, but when they hear a knock, they assume it's just the silly old neighbor and don't answer. You never know when or where big breakthroughs can come from.

"Expect the best. Prepare for the worst. Capitalize on what comes." *Zig Ziglar*

2. Maintain a positive perspective, even if things might seem less than perfect from the outside.

If you try something and it doesn't work out, don't get discouraged. Everybody has speedbumps on the road to success — the difference is whether you grow and learn from them, or give up. The seeds of luck often take time to grow.

"I have not failed. I have just found 10,000 ways that won't work." *Thomas Edison*

3. Make other people lucky

Many successful people say that the single most important investment you can make is in your relationships. So if you have the opportunity to make somebody else feel lucky, do it! By searching for ways to help others, you will often find ways to help yourself too.

"Shallow men believe in luck or in circumstance. Strong men believe in cause and effect."
Ralph Waldo Emerson

Naked Cappuccino

Two shots of Espresso, one shot of hot water, topped with frothed milk. Basically an Americano with foam... A stripped version of the cappuccino.

"People are very open-minded about new things — as long as they're exactly like the old ones." *Charles Kettering*

Next!

"Your life does not get better by chance, it gets better by change." *Jim Rohn*

If we want to be happier, healthier or more successful, we can't keep doing the same things that we always have. If we want new results, we have to try new things. When we're not living the lives we want, the answer is not always to dig in and work harder. Sometimes, we just need to take a new approach or change up the whole situation.

Studies have shown that we feel very tired and unmotivated when we are bored, but doing new things can energize and excite us. Some say we stop being curious when we get older... Or is it that we grow old when we stop being curious?

"When you're finished changing, you're finished."
Benjamin Franklin

Fika provides the perfect opportunity to practice doing new things. Sitting down with someone new in a new place with a new drink might be just what you need to pull yourself out of a slump. At worst, you don't like that person, that place or that drink, and you've lost 15 minutes. At best, well there's no limit — you might find a new best friend, business venture, favorite coffee shop, etc. The risks are not great, but the reward has the potential to be.

"If you try to fail, and succeed, which have you done?"
George Carlin

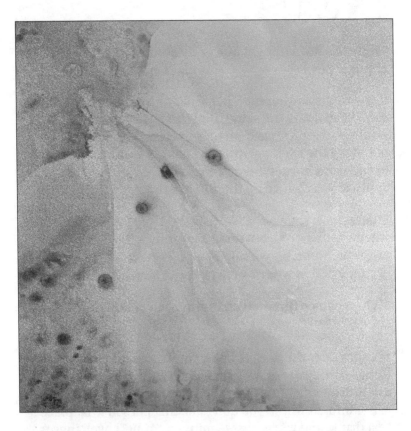

"Our dilemma is that we hate change and love it at the same time; what we really want is for things to remain the same, but get better." *Sydney J. Harris*

New life checklist

Try to check at least one item off from this list every day!
You'll be amazed at how rewarding, energizing and fun
even the smallest change can be.

I took a new route to work today ⋯⋯⋯⋯⋯⋯⋯⋯⋯⋯ ☐

I introduced myself to someone new ⋯⋯⋯⋯⋯⋯⋯⋯ ☐

I dressed myself in a new style this morning ⋯⋯⋯ ☐

I sat in a totally new spot for lunch ⋯⋯⋯⋯⋯⋯⋯ ☐

I learned a new word or interesting fact ⋯⋯⋯⋯⋯ ☐

I made / ordered a new dish for dinner ⋯⋯⋯⋯⋯ ☐

I read (at least part of) a new book ⋯⋯⋯⋯⋯⋯⋯ ☐

I greeted people in a new way ⋯⋯⋯⋯⋯⋯⋯⋯⋯ ☐

I listened to a new radio station / podcast / artist ⋯⋯ ☐

I tried a new workout ⋯⋯⋯⋯⋯⋯⋯⋯⋯⋯⋯⋯ ☐

I tried a new morning or night routine ⋯⋯⋯⋯⋯ ☐

**"All life is an experiment. The more
experiments you make, the better."**
Ralph Waldo Emerson

Organic Coffee

Organic Coffee is grown without the use of chemical fertilizers and pesticides, and therefore maintains the natural nutrients of the coffee bean. Organic Coffee is healthier for you and better for the environment than the standard bean. And if it's fair trade, it's better for the people, too!

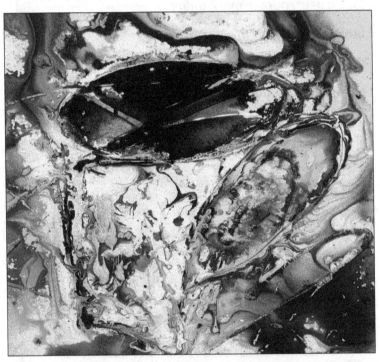

"Positive thinking is more than just a tagline. It changes the way we behave. And I firmly believe that when I am positive, it not only makes me better, but it also makes those around me better." *Harvey Mackay*

Overflow Optimism!

"I am an optimist. It does not seem much use to be anything else." *Winston Churchill*

Optimism is not just some foofy thing, it's actually a scientifically proven technique for creating a healthier, happier and wealthier life. Research found that patients who undergo heart surgery have a much higher chance of survival and shorter recovery times if they go into the procedure with positive expectations, rather than fear, worry or anger.

"Some people grumble that roses have thorns; I am grateful that thorns have roses." *Alphonse Karr*

Many people look down on optimism because they think it is based in ignorance. But, choosing to be optimistic is not at all the same as putting your head in the sand. It actually takes more work to remain positive through everything than it does to simply wallow in the misery that seems to be everywhere. We cannot help being affected by all the negative information we are constantly fed by the news, media and toxic people around us — but we don't have to swallow it all. Funny enough, we can learn a lot from dogs in this area. After all, what do dogs do after falling into a puddle? They jump back up and shake it off! We, too, can shake off the irritation, fear and worry instead of dwelling in it all day. Or like Teflon pans, we can just let the negativity slide right off us!

"Happiness is not the absence of problems, it's the ability to deal with them." *Steve Maraboli*

Paleo Coffee

Mix one tsp of Ghee and one tsp of coconut oil into your morning coffee, and feel free to add a little sugar if you prefer it. Blend all ingredients together to prevent separation and create a little layer of foam on top. Certain experts claim that this mixture gives you an extra dose of energy and clarity. At the very least, it is a tasty alternative to the usual coffee.

"And in the end, it's not the years in your life that count. It's the life in your years." *Abraham Lincoln*

Participate in the present!

"If you're reading this, congratulations, you're alive. If that's not something to smile about, I don't know what is."
Chad Sugg

Many people have difficulty enjoying life because there is always so much else to worry about. Participating in the present can be a real challenge because it's so easy to get caught up in the drama of the future or the past and forget to experience what is in front of us right now. So, many of us end up just watching life go by, rather than participating in it. At the end of the day, it feels like we were observers in our own show — and another episode just ended.

We have to be ready to go out and grab the life we want! We can't sit around hoping for "one day," when we have one day right here, right now. You don't even have to do anything crazy or revolutionary — sometimes, being present just means taking a few deep breaths, refocusing on what is in front of you right now and doing the best you can in this moment.

"The people who get most out of life are not those who lived for a century, but those who lived every minute."
Collette

Enjoy the present and find ways to help other people enjoy it, too. There will always be things to stress you out or make you feel miserable, but there will always be things to make you feel happy, loved and positive, too. Usually, those positive things are waiting for us right here and now, whereas the miserable things are waiting in the uncertainty that is yesterday or tomorrow. Take today and make it your own — you deserve it!

Queen's Cup

Two shots of espresso, one scoop of vanilla ice cream. Drizzle with maple syrup and serve in the fanciest glass available. No mugs allowed! Pinkies up.

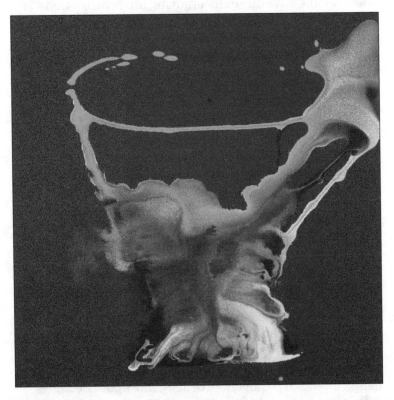

"There were some problems only coffee and ice cream could fix." *Amal El-Mohtar*

Quiet your mind!

"God is silent. Now if only man would shut up." *Woody Allen*

As much as we need to connect with others, we also need time to be quiet and connect with ourselves. Unfortunately, for many of us, it's impossible to hear our quiet, inner thoughts when the mind always talks so loud, and the world around us never stops. In this increasingly loud and interconnected world, it's very difficult to create time to settle the mind and emotions and really listen inside. Music, messaging, email, movies, you name it, are all at our fingertips. So why waste our time in silent contemplation, listening to our thoughts, when Google can give us the answers in half a second?

"It is not easy to find happiness in ourselves and it is not possible to find it elsewhere." *Agnes Reppler*

Many of the most successful and happiest people claim that their best ideas come from a place where their minds are quiet and they are just "in the zone." In order to get in that zone, many of these people dedicate a certain amount of time each day to calming the mind. Whether it's a quiet walk on the beach, some form of prayer, contemplation or meditation, or even just sitting alone for a few minutes, the key is to create some quiet time in the middle of even the craziest day.

"A happy life must be to a great extent a quiet life, for it is only in an atmosphere of quiet that true joy dares live."
Bertrand Russell

Red Eye

One cup of coffee mixed with one (or two, or three) shots of espresso. It's basically coffee mixed with more coffee... This is guaranteed to keep your red eyes wide open after taking the red eye flight. This drink is sometimes called a "shot in the dark."

"You must be shapeless, formless, like water. When you pour water in a cup, it becomes the cup. When you pour water in a bottle, it becomes the bottle. When you pour water in a teapot, it becomes the teapot. Water can drip and it can crash. Become like water, my friend." *Bruce Lee*

Roll with it!

"I am a man of fixed and unbending principles, the first of which is to be flexible at all times." *Everett Dirksen*

Many of us have a desire to control and organize everything that happens in our lives. But, at a certain point, we must choose to be flexible and willing to accept what may be beyond our control. This simple choice helps us to both focus on addressing the things that we can control, and also feel better knowing we are not responsible for the entire world.

"I have to say that I've always believed perfectionism is more of a disease than a quality. I do try to go with the flow but I can't let go." *Rowan Atkinson*

In attempting to build any sort of relationship, being able to roll with things is a crucial first step. Trying to control other people or force them to live a certain way is a recipe for disaster because they will inevitably feel smothered, and you will inevitably feel disappointed. Instead, it is wise to just roll with some things, let other people deal with their own problems, and focus on dealing with yours.

"Stay committed to your decisions, but stay flexible in your approach." *Tony Robbins*

And, as we move forward in life, toward our hopes and dreams and success, it's important to realize that change is the natural way of life. It's silly to try and force the world, or even yourself, to remain the same. Save yourself a lot of pain, stress and anger and practice rolling with the things that are beyond your control. We each have to find ways to enjoy life, and sometimes all it takes is choosing to do so.

Short Black

Double shot of espresso served in a glass.

"Life without coffee is like love without kisses." *Swedish Saying*

Stress Less – Smile More!

"I'm really exciting. I smile a lot, I win a lot, and I'm really sexy." *Serena Williams*

One of the easiest shortcuts to less stress, more happiness and better relationships is smiling! A smile is more infectious than the common cold and, instead of getting everybody sick for two weeks, your smile can actually make yourself and everybody else feel better.

"A smile is happiness you'll find right under your nose." *Tom Wilson*

We all have these things called mirror neurons in our brains that instinctively make us mirror on our own faces what we see on other peoples' faces. So, we yawn if we see someone yawn, tear up if we see someone cry, or smile if we see someone smile. We are biologically wired to share in other peoples' emotions. So do everybody a favor and smile! Let others share in your joy.

"Practice smiling. Smile at lampposts and mailboxes. Don't be modest — this isn't the time." *Jacque Mercer*

Life is so much more fun when we relax and focus on reasons to smile, rather than frown. Many people are so easily angered or offended because they walk around with a chip on their shoulder, assuming that the world is out to get them. But once we realize that the world is not actually against us — and that it is totally okay that not everyone shares the same opinions, taste, or sense of humor — life suddenly feels full of reasons to smile.

A simple smile can....

> **Boost your mood**
> **Cut your stress level**
> **Lower your heart rate**
> **Reduce your pain**
> **Help you be more attractive**
> **Make you look younger**
> **Boost your immune system**

"A smile is the light in your window that tells others that there is a caring, sharing person inside."
Denis Waitley

"We shall never know all the good a simple smile can do."

Mother Teresa

Turkish Coffee

Grind your beans extra fine. Place 1.5 tbsp of ground coffee, a small pinch of cardamom and another of cinnamon, and sugar to taste into one cup of water and heat over medium heat in a saucepan. Do not stir yet. When you see the mix is on the verge of boiling, turn the heat to low. Begin to stir the brew with a spoon or whisk to build the signature 'foam' of Turkish Coffee. If it starts to boil, remove from heat for a few moments to cool it down and repeat the process. Pour into fancy cups and enjoy! *Do not drink the coffee grounds at the bottom – let it settle for at least a minute before drinking.

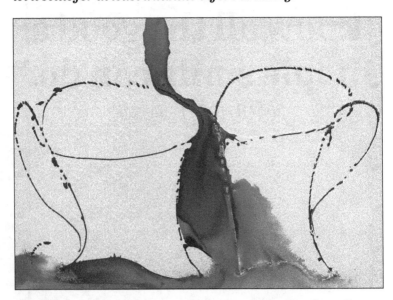

"Coffee should be black as hell, strong as death and sweet as love." *Turkish Proverb*

Trust Yourself!

"I am not bound to win, but I am bound to be true. I am not bound to success, but I am bound to live by the light that I have. I must stand with anybody that stands right, and stand with him while he is right, and part with him when he goes wrong." *Abraham Lincoln*

When people think of honesty and character, we most often think of how other people see us, and sometimes we're even willing to lie in order to make other people think us honest and moral — it's kind of crazy. But, most of the time, the only person you're truly accountable to is yourself. Some people view that as a free pass to play hookie and get away with anything; but, there's always a part of us watching for this. There's just no escaping yourself.

"Well, if you're true to yourself you're going to be true to everyone else." *John Wooden*

If we want to live happy, successful and fulfilled lives, we have to be able to trust all parts of ourselves. And as we build this trust within ourselves, the feeling of trustworthiness naturally flows out from us into the relationships all around us. Businesses bloom, relationships thrive and everything benefits when we operate from a level of honesty. Where the truth is involved, confidence follows. The self-confidence, love and respect that come from the commitment to be trustworthy are more valuable than almost anything an object, person or situation could give you.

"I'm killing time while I wait for life to shower me with meaning and happiness." *Bill Watterson*

Unfiltered Coffee

*A very simple way to make a good, strong cuppa. Place four tsp of finely ground coffee per cup of water into a pot. Bring to a boil. Pour into a cup and drink. *Do not drink coffee grounds – let settle one minute before drinking.*

"No one can understand the truth until he drinks a coffee's frothy goodness." *Sheikh Abd-Al-Kadir*

Understand That You Don't Understand!

Many people go through life feeling upset at anything that doesn't fit within their picture of how the world should be — and it's a huge waste of time and energy. We spend so much of our life feeling resentful or upset that things are not how we want them to be, when we could be spending that time actually doing something to make the world a better place.

"Wise men don't need advice. Fools won't take it."
Benjamin Franklin

Do you want to create a lifestyle that puts the fun in functional? The first step is to approach each day, each moment with the understanding that you simply do not understand. Remember that puppy-eyed sense of wonder that we couldn't seem to contain as children? That joyful embrace of the novelty of the universe seems to vanish as soon as we start looking at ourselves as *smart, wise, adult*, or whatever we want to call it. But, when we let go of trying to prove just how *smart, wise*, and *adult* we are, and just love life for what it is, the world seems so much more magical and friendly.

"The only true wisdom is in knowing you know nothing."
Socrates

We need to keep our eyes on the bigger picture and weed out a lot of our own useless worrying. Use your heart, your inner wisdom and your sense of wonder to find that feeling of joy that comes with understanding the bigger picture.

"Knowledge is knowing that a tomato is a fruit, wisdom is not putting it in a fruit salad." *Brian O'Driscoll*

Vienna

Pour two shots of espresso into a fancy glass and mix with steamed milk. Whip one cup of whipping cream, ½ tsp of vanilla extract and 1 tbsp of sugar in a mixing bowl until it reaches a fairly thick consistency. Top the coffee with a dollop of vanilla cream and a dusting of unsweetened cocoa powder.

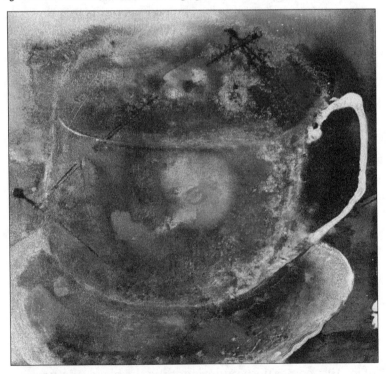

"In my mind, I've always been an A-list Hollywood super-star. Y'all just didn't know it yet." *Will Smith*

Visualize Victory!

"Hold the image of your success and your completion in front of you, and keep moving forward. It will becomes obvious, moment to moment, what must be done next."
John Roger

From daily success to lifelong goals, visualization is an extremely effective technique. World famous athletes visualize their success before a game. The best speakers in the world visualize an engaged and excited crowd before they go out. Actors, musicians, businesspeople, etc. all do this in their own way. A few moments of positive visualization can really help you succeed in all different areas of life.

"It is true of the Nation, as of the individual, that the greatest doer must also be a great dreamer."
Theodore Roosevelt

Still, some people say they do not want to celebrate things in advance, in case they never happen — yet so many of us constantly worry and stress about things in the future that will probably never happen! We are willing to engage in negative visualization all the time, but we hesitate to engage in positive visualization. It's a strange double standard that can be really damaging to your health, wealth, happiness and success.

"I've had a lot of worries in my life, most of which never happened." *Mark Twain*

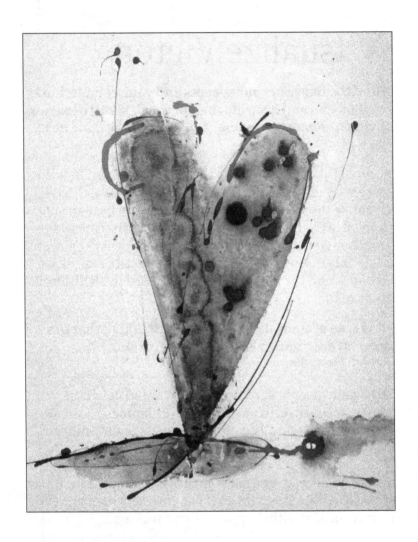

"If you don't know where you're going, any road will take you there." *Lewis Carroll*

Visualization is the real deal. *Try this!* Next time you have a task to accomplish, take 10 seconds beforehand and visualize what it would feel like if you did it absolutely perfectly. What would you do to celebrate? How would everyone else react? How would you feel? If you want to accomplish something, set a clear intention of getting it done with fun and ease, instead of just dreading another day at work or another chore. Run these images and feelings through your head before you start, and watch the results flow.

"You can have anything you want if you want it badly enough. You can be anything you want to be, do anything you set out to accomplish if you hold to that desire with singleness of purpose." *Abraham Lincoln*

In visualization, the more specific you can get, the more effective you will be. Answer these questions to build your crystal clear vision of your life goal:

1. What does your perfect week look like? No boundaries, no limits.

2. What does your perfect lifestyle entail? Lots of travel? Time off? Fame? Competition? Family?

3. Where does your ideal self live? What are the aromas in the air there? What kind of neighbors do you have?

4. What is your ideal self wearing? What do you smell like? What colors are you in?

5. What kinds of things would you do every day if you had your choice and no restrictions?

6. Combine these answers into a cohesive picture or narrative in your head. Try to actually feel, smell, hear, see, etc. the things you would if you were living the dream.

White Chocolate Latte

One-half cup whole milk, one tsp heavy cream, one tsp sugar. Combine ingredients in sauce pan. Heat and stir until hot and frothy. Pour into mug with two shots of espresso, and handful of white chocolate chips (to taste) and a dash of vanilla extract.

"I think if I were a woman, I'd wear coffee as a perfume."
John VanDruten

Wow Them!

We all have to accept that it's up to us to make the most of the cards we're dealt. As much as life happens to us, we can happen to life! We each have power to affect change if we want to – we can all be winners if we really, truly want to be, and are willing to sacrifice to get there.

"You have to take 100% responsibility for everything that you experience in your life." *Jack Canfield*

When we own our power and decide to be winners, we inevitably feel better about ourselves and have more confidence to reach out and connect to others. As we stop fearing setbacks, problems and stress — and instead look at them as opportunities and inspiration to be more creative — life opens itself up to us, and connections, success and happiness just seem to flow in.

"In all of living, have much fun and laughter. Life is to be enjoyed, not just endured." *Gordon B. Hinckley*

We each have our own unique, incredible qualities — sometimes, we just have to look really hard to find them. Answer these questions to give yourself a head start toward finding your own, personal Wow Factors!

Find Your Wow Factors!
Just answer the following questions

1. As a child, what did you dream about being as a grownup?

"Adults are always asking kids what they want to be when they grow up because they are looking for ideas."
Paula Poundstone

2. What would you want to do, if money and recognition were irrelevant to your decision?

"My mission in life is not merely to survive, but to thrive; and to do so with some passion, some compassion, some humor, and some style." *Maya Angelou*

3. Who do you admire? Why? What do these people represent that you would like to develop in yourself?

"My mother said to me, 'If you are a soldier, you will become a general. If you are a monk, you will become the Pope.' Instead I was a painter and became Picasso."
Pablo Picasso

4. Ask yourself *Why?* What motivates you? What is your real goal?

"He who has a why can bear almost any how." *Nietzsche*

5. Is there a cause you feel strongly for? Is there a difference you would like to make in the world?

"If you love your work, you'll be out there every day trying to do it the best you possibly can, and pretty soon everybody around will catch the passion from you – like a fever." *Sam Walton*

6. How do you want people to tell your story?

"The difference between ordinary and extraordinary is that little extra." *Jimmy Johnson*

Xtra Strong Coffee

Add a scoop of collagen or protein powder to your morning coffee to get an xtra good, supercharged start to your day!

Actually, this seems to be the basic need of the human heart in nearly every great crisis – a good, hot cup of coffee" *Alexander King*

Leave your e**X**es in the past!

"Forgiveness does not change the past, but it does enlarge the future." *Paul Boose*

Never think of yourself as an ex anything! It's easy to fall into the *shoulda, coulda, woulda* mentality when we think of our past, but that can be really draining. Think of your energy as a flashlight — you have to shine it where you want to go. If you're constantly shining it where you've been, how can you see where you're going? The trick is to forgive, learn, forget and move on.

"Holding a grudge is like drinking poison and waiting for the other person to die." *William Shakespeare*

We have to invest in the future, not the past. Living in the glory or drama of the past can never bring any real level of peace or satisfaction. It's like trying to cook a gourmet dinner with an old, spoiled piece of meat — no matter how you season it, it's never going to taste good. Don't expect your life to feel good, either, if you hold onto old, spoiled habits, memories and grudges.

"Yesterday is not ours to recover, but tomorrow is ours to win or lose." *Lyndon B. Johnson*

Yeunyeung

Mix two cups of coffee with one cup of black tea, ½ cup of whole milk and two tsp sugar. Can be served either hot or chilled. This Hong Kong classic is named after the Mandarin duck Yuenyeung because the male and female look so different and, thus, embody the idea that opposites attract — just like coffee and tea in this drink!

"Persist — don't take no for an answer. If you're happy to sit at your desk and not take any risk, you'll be sitting at your desk for the next 20 years." *David Rubenstein*

Yes!

"You can't prevent birds of sorrow from flying over your head. But you can prevent them from building a nest in your hair." *Chinese Proverb*

One of the most crucial aspects of a happy, healthy life is the understanding that it's up to you to find your *Yes!* in life, and each *no* that you get is just a step toward that *Yes!* Almost every *no* that you hear is neither personal nor final. There are thousands of reasons why someone might say *no* today and then *Yes!* tomorrow. Research agrees: according to market studies, prospective buyers need to hear about a product roughly seven times before they actually buy it. Does that mean they hated the product the first six times they heard about it? Of course not! They just weren't ready to say *Yes!* the first time around.

"I have enjoyed life a lot more by saying 'Yes' than by saying 'No.'" *Richard Branson*

Successful, happy people look at rejections as opportunities to improve, rather than reasons to quit. So next time you feel rejected, ask the person rejecting you what it would take to earn a *Yes!* and use that feedback to grow.

"Nothing in this world can take the place of persistence. Talent will not: nothing is more common than unsuccessful men with talent. Genius will not; unrewarded genius is almost a proverb. Education will not: the world is full of educated derelicts. Persistence and determination alone are omnipotent." *Calvin Coolidge*

"The big question is whether you are going to be able to say a hearty yes to your adventure." *Joseph Campbell*

Can you imagine where we would be if everybody who was rejected actually quit?

"We don't like their sound, and guitar music is on it's way out." *Decca Recording Company rejecting the Beatles, 1962*

Lincoln lost 8 elections and suffered a nervous breakdown before becoming president.

Harry Potter was rejected 12 times, Gone With the Wind 38 times and Chicken Soup for the Soul 144 times.

"The difference between the possible and the impossible lies in a person's determination." *Tommy Lasorda*

Zestpresso

Grind a little bit of nutmeg, cinnamon and cloves into your coffee grinds before brewing. Or, if you buy pre-ground, just add the spices into the mixture. Start out very light with the spices and add more if you need it. This drink is sure to add some excitement to your morning with no extra calories or sugar.

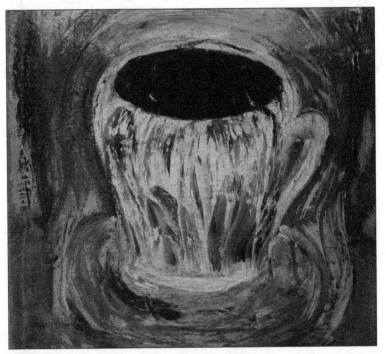

"If you have zest and enthusiasm, you attract zest and enthusiasm. Life does give back in kind."
Norman Vincent Peale

Zest it up!

Life is ours for the taking! So why take it slow, sad and simple? Search for ways to fill your days with color, beauty, grace, excitement or whatever makes you feel alive!

"Zest is the secret of all beauty. There is no beauty that is attractive without zest." *Christian Dior*

Most people are afraid to be zesty or express themselves honestly because they fear what other people will think. But most people are so bored and zoned out that they would love to just meet an interesting person, or even see somebody doing something interesting — they don't have any interest in judging you! And, even if they did, what's the difference to you if Frank from Delaware thinks you're boring? (Nothing against you, hypothetical Frank from Delaware.) Don't be afraid to be the center of attention — you just might be the light that brightens up somebody's day.

"Choosing the freedom to be uninteresting never quite worked for me." *Diane Keaton*

Each of us can be a leader by just bringing a little bit of zest and positivity to the table every day, even if it's just about simple things, like beautiful weather or light traffic. We are magnets, and we attract what we focus on. So, if you want to feel good, focus on the good in yourself and others. Enthusiasm is contagious, after all, so why not be someone you would want to be around, yourself? You just might find that other people want to be around you, too!

"An entire sea of water can't sink a ship unless it gets inside the ship. Similarly, the negativity of the world can't put you down unless you allow it to get inside you."
Goi Nasu

"Thousands of candles can be lighted from a single candle, and the life of the candle will not be shortened. Happiness never decreases by being shared." *Buddha*

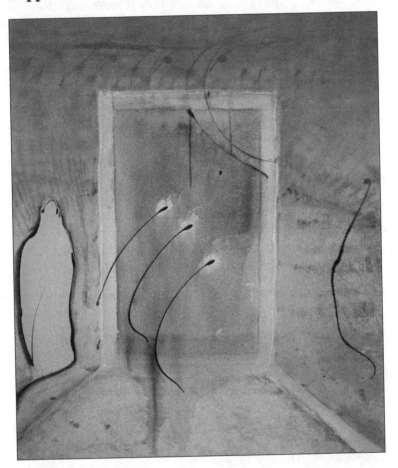

"We must let go of the life we have planned, so as to accept the one that is waiting for us." *Joseph Campbell*

What comes after the end?

In the Swedish Alphabet, Z is followed by three more letters: Å, Ä and Ö.

If you feel depressed because something is ending, it's a good idea to remind yourself that there is always more to come. What looks like the end might actually be the beginning of something you didn't see coming before — something new, something better.

"Be open to what comes next for you. You may be heading in one direction and then life brings you another that might be a good thing." *Natalie Cane*

At a certain point, we have to make a conscious decision to focus on taking care of ourselves before we try to solve all the problems of the past and the whole world. What good is it to walk around feeling miserable, with our minds racing about world peace? We have a responsibility to take care of ourselves — for our own sakes, and for our communities' sakes — so that nobody else has to. We have to do our best to feel, think and be our best so that we can then put forward our best efforts to improve the world.

"My therapist told me the way to achieve true inner peace is to finish what I start. So far, I have finished two bags of M&Ms and chocolate cake. I feel better already."
Dave Barry

With the last three letters in this alphabet, you will find recipes for three of our favorite Swedish baked goods. These three are sure to stand out at any bake sale, Fika or special event. So please enjoy and remember to share!

Kladdkaka

Gluten Free, low on sugar and absolutely incredible!

Ingredients:

3 eggs

1.5 cups sugar

½ tsp salt

1 tsp vanilla extract

5 tbsp cocoa powder

2 tsp strong coffee

½ cup whole milk

150 g melted butter

Make it happen!

1. Whisk the eggs and sugar together until they have a nice airiness about them.
2. Gently stir in salt, vanilla, cocoa and flour until uniform in color and consistency.
3. Gently mix in coffee, milk and butter.
4. Pour mix into a buttered, round pie dish.

Bake!

Set the oven to 350° F and bake for 30-35 minutes
The cake is ready when it's just a little gooey, but not wet.

Enjoy!

Serve at room temperature or chilled with some whipped cream, berries, bananas or peaches.

Åk! .... Go!

Åk, means go or keep going! When the quiet Swede Ingemar Stenmark — regarded as the greatest slalom and giant slalom specialist of all time — was asked what his secret was, he answered, "Det är bara å åk!" Which means "It is only to GO!"

"Go for it now. The future is promised to no one."
Wayne Dyer

Stenmark's answer highlights such a simple, but profound truth. Just go for it! Whatever it is that you'd like to do! If you want to talk to someone new, dress differently or help someone, just GO FOR IT! Do not overthink, waste time worrying or let your fear of rejection stop you from making things happen. Only by going for it can you create the life you deserve!

"Keep on going and the chances are you will stumble on something, perhaps when you are least expecting it. I have never heard of anyone stumbling on something sitting down." *Charles Kettering*

Always keep on going. When you reach your goal, say, *Next!* Don't settle for mediocracy. Go for it! Travel, explore, investigate, question! Fill your life with enthusiasm and things that push you forward.

Schackrutor

Egg free, beautiful and absolutely delicious.

General Ingredients:
2.25 cups flour
½ cup sugar
½ tsp salt
200g room temp. butter

Brown:
2 tbsp cocoa powder

White:
1.5 tsp vanilla extract
(2tsp vanilla sugar is ideal)

Make it happen!

Mix the "general ingredients" in a bowl. Separate the dough into two equal amounts and place into separate bowls. Add "white" and "brown" ingredients to separate bowls. Mix! Take the white dough and split it into two. Work each half into a long, rectangular loaf. Repeat this step with the brown half. Once you have four little loaves, stack them 2x2 to create the checkerboard effect. Push gently on each side of the combined loaf to make sure the different colors stick together through baking. Cut the cookies into ½ - ¾ inch slices and place on a baking sheet.

Bake!

350° F for 10-12 minutes. Cookies should be soft, not mushy.

Älska!  Love!

"If you would be loved, love and be lovable." *Benjamin Franklin*

Love is the force that lets us transform our lives from mediocre to extraordinary, but often we trade in that incredible power of love for something much less valuable. We excuse ourselves because we have too much to do to take the time to make the people in our lives feel that they are seen, heard and appreciated.

"Before you marry a person, you should first make them use a computer with slow internet service to see who they really are." *Will Ferrell*

To be loving in how we speak is good — to be loving in how we act is even better. Loving someone means taking action each day, not just on special occasions with the huge romantic gestures. The real love lives within all the small, simple actions, like getting up to greet a family member when they enter your home, acknowledging a coworker's efforts or bringing a friend a cup of coffee now and then.

"We waste time looking for the perfect lover, instead of creating the perfect love." *Tom Robbins*

Love songs are usually not about visiting your grandma or playing chess with an old neighbor, but that type of loving is just as important as the romantic kind. By becoming more caring and loving people, we also attract more caring and loving people into our lives.

"Love is an act of endless forgiveness, a tender look which becomes a habit." *Peter Ustinov*

157

Chokladbollar

Egg & Gluten free, No-Bake, Unbelievably Addictive!

Ingredients:
100g room temp. butter
1 tbsp cocoa powder
4 tbsp sugar
1.25 cups rolled oatmeal
1 tbsp strong coffee

Toppings:
Pearl sugar
Coconut
Walnuts
Anything you like!

Make it happen!
Thoroughly mix all the ingredients (not toppings) in a bowl. Roll bite-size balls of the mix with your hands and place upon a plate. Roll the balls around in the toppings of your choice. Refrigerate for at least 30 minutes.

Enjoy!
Eat up! There's no wrong way to enjoy a chokladboll.

Island

"We are like islands in the sea, separate on the surface but connected in the deep." *William James*

It's easy to get caught up in the illusion of separation when we are stressed out — many of us seem to forget that we're even on the same planet. It helps to remind ourselves that, just like islands, we are all connected to one another...Sometimes, we just have to look a little deeper to realize that.

"The one thing that unites all human beings, regardless of age, gender, religion, economic status, or ethnic background, is that, deep down inside, we all believe that we are above-average drivers." *Dave Barry*

Our belief is that if more people were willing to take the time to connect with others each day — whether it's just a 15-minute Fika or greeting a coworker with a smile — we would learn to see that we truly are all connected, and none of us are alone.

"Students achieving oneness will move on to twoness."
Woody Allen

Section #6:

Join the Fika Force!

"Never underestimate the power of dreams and the influence of the human spirit. We are all the same in this notion: The potential for greatness lives within each of us."

Wilma Rudolph

The Long Distance Farmer

An old farmer lived on a farm in Idaho with his son. One year, just before potato planting season, the son was wrongfully arrested for robbing a bank.

As planting time grew closer and closer, the old man began to panic. "Dear son," he wrote, "I don't know what to do. I'm far too old to dig up this field myself, and without this harvest I'm going to lose the farm. I miss you. Love, Dad."

A few days later, the old man received a letter from his son... "Dear dad, we can't dig there anyway. That's where I buried all the money from the bank! Don't worry, we'll use that to cover all of our costs."

The very next day, while the old man sat with his morning coffee, the entire county's police force came rushing onto his farm, sirens blaring. Without so much as glancing at the old farmer, they began to furiously rip his fields apart, looking for the money. By nightfall, every inch of the farm had been dug up, but no money had been found.

The next morning, another letter arrived: "There you go, Dad. Go ahead and plant your potatoes now. It's the best I could do from here. Love, your son."

"If opportunity doesn't knock, build a door."

Milton Berle

If there's one thing we hope you've learned by reading this book — aside from how to have Fika, of course — it's that we all have the power to find solutions to whatever our problems might be. Just like the son in jail, we all can find the way to our goals and dreams if we decide to approach life with an unshakeable sense of creativity and enthusiasm.

As you move onward and upward from here, remember that there is always hope, there is always opportunity, and you never have to be the victim of your circumstances. You are powerful, capable and important, and that is as good a reason as any to smile, if you ask us.

Onward & Upward

We hope that you have enjoyed reading *Fika That!* as much as we've enjoyed writing it. It's always tough to finish reading a book that you've enjoyed, but the great thing about this book is that the real fun begins now!

Now you have all the tools, information and insights you need to join the Fika Force and start making this world a more connected, loving and understanding place — all through the power of Fika. And the best part is that you can do this and transform your life, and the lives of the people around you, in just 15 minutes per day.

Our last piece of advice to you, on your journey to creating your best life, is this: Don't sleep on things for too long. When you feel inspired, when the idea is fresh in your mind, act! You're minutes away from finishing this book — why not call up an old friend and schedule a Fika? What better time is there than right now? Go for it!

Once again, *thank you* for choosing to work toward a happier, more connected future with us. We hope to have Fika with you soon!

With Love and Coffee,
Émile and Åsa

For more about this project, other projects, speaking & coaching, or to contact us visit...

FikaThat.com

Meet Åsa Odbäck

Åsa Odbäck grew up in Sweden, where she graduated #1 in her class from Law School, after which she taught law at the University of Stockholm before proceeding to graduate #1 from Stockholm Business School. She then founded a major success training firm that worked with international companies like Volvo and Ericsson. Later, she served as head of Press and Information for the Swedish Defense University before moving to California where she raised three boys (one of whom she wrote this book with), authored five books and started a company to support female artists. While fighting a serious illness, Åsa used art and connection to heal her body and heart, and has since created over 200 paintings, and endless Fikas.

AsaKatarina.com

Meet Émile Odbäck

Émile graduated from the University of California Santa Barbara with highest honors and a University Award of Distinction, as a member of the Phi Beta Kappa Honors Society, and was selected to give the graduation speech for nearly 10,000 people. While at UCSB, Émile served as the Editor in Chief of the University's top-nationally-ranked Newspaper, the Daily Nexus, where he won several awards and broke a story that helped a political refugee gain asylum in the United States. Also, in his time off, Émile worked with a top Hollywood director, and published a book on student success. Émile now speaks to thousands of students per year, and works full time to help people relearn the art and importance of connection — often by sharing Fika!

EmileOdback.com

CPSIA information can be obtained
at www.ICGtesting.com
Printed in the USA
FSHW01n0000090818
51180FS